My Conversations with Canadians

FIRST EDITION

Third printing

The production of this book was made possible through the generous assistance of the Canada Council for the Arts and the Ontario Arts Council. BookThug also acknowledges the support of the Government of Canada through the Canada Book Fund and the Government of Ontario through the Ontario Book Publishing Tax Credit and the Ontario Book Fund.

BookThug acknowledges the land on which it operates. For thousands of years it has been the traditional land of the Huron-Wendat, the Seneca, and most recently, the Mississaugas of the Credit River. Today, this meeting place is still the home to many Indigenous people from across Turtle Island and we are grateful to have the opportunity to work on this land.

LIBRARY AND ARCHIVES CANADA CATALOGUING IN PUBLICATION

Maracle, Lee, 1950–
[Essays. Selections]
    My conversations with Canadians / Lee Maracle.

(Essais ; no. 4)
Issued in print and electronic formats.
softcover: ISBN 978-1-77166-358-8
html: ISBN 978-1-77166-359-5
pdf: ISBN 978-1-77166-360-1
kindle: ISBN 978-1-77166-361-8

 I. Title. II. Series: Essais (Toronto, Ont.) ; no. 4

PS8576.A6175A6 2017   C814'.54   C2017-904674-8   C2017-904675-6

PRINTED IN CANADA

My Conversations with Canadians

Lee Maracle

BookThug
Toronto, 2017
Essais no. 4

Conversations:

Conversation 1:
Meeting the public

You are always sitting just out of reach of my kitchen table; you occupy a large space in my mind, and so I thought I would like to have a conversation with you. You are not invited into the text to respond, and for that I apologize. Instead I take it upon myself to scribble a number of chapters in response to a number of common questions. I hope to create a conversational book. Perhaps we will meet at some justice event in the future. But now, in my imagination, I locate you in my kitchen. I am living in a co-op, the first Indigenous co-op in Western Canada. The women own the units and we were influential in the design of the kitchen, living, dining rooms. This is a long kitchen/dining space bordered by windows at one end and stove, fridge, sink, and cupboards at the other. I have papered the wall halfway up in the seating area with wallpaper that is very much like the cloth I use in my quilt making. We are seated around my oak table with its ten chairs. It is an antique. It took twelve years for me to be able to afford this table. The children are in the living room, down the hall from the kitchen. This is so they can play undisturbed but be heard from the kitchen while the women gather around the kitchen table to plan the transformation of the world, so to speak. I drop a cup of coffee on the table and begin these conversations that I would like to have with you.

I have seen many of you at book launches, panels, conferences, gatherings of all sorts, including protests against some injustice or other of which there are so many. Not a single Canadian has ever approached me to say: "Why are there so many injustices committed against Indigenous people?" or "Why is there not a strong movement of support for justice and sovereignty for Indigenous people's sovereignty movement in Canada?" Canadians love causes, but they love the causes that are far away—out of their backyard, so to speak.

Oh, wait: they don't actually have a legitimate backyard. They are here at our goodwill and by our host laws and by way of honouring our treaties—should that happen. Most Canadians don't see it that way, however. Nothing that happens to Indigenous people, no matter how unlawful, is of much consequence to many of the people occupying Indigenous territories. In fact, just the other day, several police officers were suspended for sexually and physically abusing Indigenous women in Peterborough. While no charges were laid—due to lack of evidence (this usually means the women themselves were the only evidence, and of course, they are not normally considered credible witnesses when facing white men, particularly police)—there was sufficient evidence to suspend them. The community came out and demonstrated in favour of the police—unprecedented. No other women are regarded in this fashion. Being a feminist, I await a feminist reaction—none. Again, unprecedented. It is as if no one cares.

We occupied this entire continent before the newcomers came. The border between the United States and Canada is an arbitrary one and it was only recently established—1812, I believe, before Canada was Canada. Many of our nations straddle this border and live on both sides. When Britain handed the reins to Upper Canada, the new country called itself Canada. In the early period of confederation we were named as permanent immigrants to Canada. They first named us permanent immigrants to Canada, then wards of the state, children in the eyes of the law, incapable of making adult decisions, and finally we became citizens. These were all arbitrary decisions made by your various governments at various times and applied to us without consultation or choice. We were not permitted to vote. Now, everyone knows this is not Europe, it is not England, or France. It is not China, India, or Africa. So how did our land get to be a country called Canada without our consent?

Further, many Canadians, when asking questions about us, refer to us as "our Natives," "our Indigenous people." You consider us your possessions at best; at worst we are like a personal footnote to the Canada that is owned by Canadians. When did we ever agree to all this?

Canadians talk *about* us oftener than *to* us. Even when they are speaking directly to us, they refer to "the Indians" of the "First Nations" as though I was not First Nations. The worst insult is being labeled with the possessive "our First Nations" as though they owned us. The conversation about us goes on in a language of possession and distancing that no one thinks about and yet everyone is shocked at the myriad of injustices visited upon our persons every day—except for the injustice that begins with the story: "It all started one day when Christopher Columbus landed a ship and asked to dock. The Indians said yes, and then Columbus drove a flag into the ground and established ownership of the Indies for

9

the queen of Spain." Less than a hundred years later, some captain did the same in Canada for the French Crown, then another captain drove his flag into the ground in the name of the British Crown, and everyone thinks that was all it took to establish Canada as a colony of England or France—depending on your national persuasion. You are convinced this is all yours and that we are a footnote owned by you.

Your previous governments secured this country by hook and by crook. These "newfound" lands cost Indigenous people their lives. Headhunting and epidemics were the forces most commonly used. Now by policing that is so chronic and relentless it feels like a solid wall of semi-military occupation: Canada controls us instead of protecting us. Not a single Canadian has ever asked me how this happened without our consent. Couple this with the majority population's accepted belief that this is all good and proper, and you have summed up Canadian colonial strategy.

We cannot say no to the development and rape of the land or our persons. We have been infantilized and animalized and finally objectified and commodified. Canadians are horrified at some of the answers to their questions: "No," they blurt out, and then they gasp. That is just annoying. Sometimes they say, "I don't understand." "Actually," I answer, "you do. This is English, this is your language." They admit that they do understand, but they are shocked. It is the shock of the innocent.

Canadians have a myth about themselves, and it seems this myth is inviolable. They are innocent. They gave us things; they were kind to us. The reality is that Canada has seized vast land tracts, leaving only small patches of land specifically for us, as though they indeed owned everything and we had nothing, not even a tablespoon of dirt. Canada says it gave us these lands, and Canadians actually believe that Canada "gave us" these reserves. In fact, Canada took all the land but the reserves it set aside for us. You cannot give someone something that already belongs to them.

There are a number of treaties between Indigenous people and Canada. The treaties between Canada and us don't say that we own nothing and Canada owns everything; in fact, they imply the opposite: Canada gets to be Canada by meeting its treaty obligations. That is, you get to be here, at our good grace and our goodwill, not the other way around.

Nor do the treaties say we do not get to be ourselves. Most of the treaties attest to our right to hunt and fish. And they accord us education rights. Some promise us homes, others say the "canoe will never be empty," and at least one says the treaty payments will go up as the income from land secession rises. There could be no hunting or fishing guarantees unless the treaty makers had recognized our original freedom of access to our ancestral lands. They show that we had the absolute right to continue to provide for our lineages. Canada just doesn't behave in accordance with the treaties' intent. It does not say in the treaties that should we change our way of sustaining ourselves, we will be violating Canadian law. They knew we occupied this land. They knew that it was the land that sustained us. The hunting and fishing rights affirm uninterrupted dominion and economic access to our original territories or treaty lands.

We know the land will continue to sustain us. The only difference in our lives is that we would have new neighbours and in exchange for sharing the land with them, we would receive some of the benefits they bring without payment from us. So-called fishing and hunting rights are just a nod to the already-existing authority we had over our land. Fishing and hunting are all we have left of our economic rights to access the wealth of our land. They are the cost to the settlers for having been granted permission to live here. The treaties outline the newcomers' obligation to us and the land as the cost of that permission.

In many treaties, the British wrote about the notion of "surrender[ing] to the crown all lands," etc. Few of our elders tell that version of the story; most say that through the treaties, the Indigenous nations allowed white people to live here. If we had surrendered our lands, there would be no "hunting or fishing rights" contained in the treaties. The hunting and fishing rights presume our uninterrupted and total economic access to the wealth of treaty lands. For more on treaties, read Harold Johnson's 2007 book, *Two Families: Treaties and Government*.

I did not know very many Canadians well when I began my writing career, or, I should say, reading and public speaking career. In fact, I wasn't even aware I would have to meet the public with my book when I began touring for *Bobbi Lee: Indian Rebel* in 1975. Book writing and publishing is definitely a Canadian cultural phenomenon. My editor told me I would have to "tour the book." "And do what?" I asked. "Read from it." "Do you really think that people who cannot read are going to buy a book?" I asked. "No," he answered, chuckling, "they can all read." "Then they can read it their own damn selves," I snipped. "You really don't know anything about publishing, do you?" he said, and laughed out loud. "Apparently not," I answered, somewhat humbled.

No one I knew had ever published anything. I take that back. I had met Malcolm Lowry, who lived on a houseboat off our reserve at Cate's Park, but I did not know he had published anything until I was nearly forty years old and I was asked to read for the Under the Volcano Festival of Art and Social Change. I knew him as Malcolm, a friendly old white man who liked me to visit. He would ask me to tell him a story, and I would, and always when I left, he would say, "Go to school and when you learn to read, you write them stories down," and he would laugh. I did not write down the ones I told him but I did want to be a writer by the time I went to college. It surprised me that my Malcolm was the author of *Under the Volcano*, which I had read.

The first reading I did was in Vancouver (or at least that is what my memory is telling me now). It was not all that important to me, this business of reading. I was mildly terrified. I did not shake, nor show my fear—not the Sto:lo way. It is our way to calm ourselves. Once we have committed to doing something, we do it with courage and conviction. Standing up and shaking is not the way to go once you have agreed to read to everyone. I recall thinking, it isn't like you are going to stumble over the words, and they are, after all, your own. And it wasn't as if I didn't know the story that was my own too. But I was cognizant that this was not my culture and that I did not know anything about it, so there could be all sorts of traps I could get caught in. I persuaded myself that might be fun too; after all, I like laughing, even if I am at the center of the joke.

Lately my audiences have been largely women of colour, Indigenous women, and white women, with a few men salting the group. Not so in the early seventies. There were a lot of men; in fact, they were mostly white men, with a few men of colour peppering the audience. I read from the first and last chapter of *Bobbi Lee*, a habit I maintained until I published with Cormorant Books, who suggested I treat the book like a script, and my editor separated out a script-sized chunk of chapter one from *Celia's Song* for me. I was not an actor then, that came much later, when my kids roped me into it. At the end of my reading of *Bobbi Lee*, the audience was invited to ask questions. "Who wrote it for you?" was a common question, asked of me as though I could not possibly have written my book myself. I half wondered how they knew very few of us could write. Or was it based on some racial dumbing down of the possibility of writing developing among us? Those kinds of questions annoy Canadians when I tell them that they were asked of me in the early days of my writing, but actually I liked them; they are so easy to answer. "No one—I wrote it myself, but I did not edit it."

About halfway through the question-and-answer period, an older man got up and bellowed out his question: "What are you going to do with us white guys—drive us into the sea?" He shook his fist. I stared at him for a while, thinking. On the one hand, there is this business of his fear, which affects so many white people here in North America. In so many movies, the line "We are in Indian country now" pops up when the heroes enter enemy territory, no matter what country the enemy is from. This is particularly true for Westerns and Vietnam War movies, but it is also true for cop shows and other war movies as well. "Indian country" is dangerous country, full of ambushes, secrecy, guerrilla fighters, traps, and maybe even some torture. I am not sure if any of this fear is grounded in reality, but I do know that a few of us gave both Canada and America a very hard time in their pursuit of subduing us and establishing the two aforementioned countries on this continent.

Hence the treaties. But that is not all. Although we gave the British and the French a hard time, we did not have genocide as a goal. Canada and the U. S. did have genocide as a goal.

14

"Nits breed lice" was General Armstrong Custer's famous line when the American army killed everyone at Wounded Knee. During the beginning period of residential school, when Dr. Bryce complained to the Superintendent of Indian Affairs that the children were all dying of disease, the superintendent's response was "If they are dying, isn't that the point?" Does the man asking me what we're going to do about white guys know about General Custer? Does he believe we are angry enough about the first forty years of residential school child killing that we want to drive him into the sea?

I didn't know the answer to his question and I didn't say anything right away. I don't remember what popped up in my mind then, but I suspected that it required a much longer answer than what I was able to give him at the time. Did he think we hated them for taking our land, for confining us to reservations, for deliberately impoverishing us? Or was it something simpler: Canadians hate Indians so we also hate them; they don't want us here and so we naturally don't want them here.

Or is there a hundred-year-old fear hidden in that question? I do recall white children telling their teacher that it was not fair to have to compete with me because I was an Indian and everyone knows Indians are better at sports and stupider in class than white kids. Was this it? He was older than me, so maybe the creepy racism of the forties and fifties had filled him with that sort of nonsense. Or was he just being insulting, letting me know he believed me to be savage and brutal, not genteel like a white girl?

In any case, this was not a simple question, but we were running short of time and I suspected that I could not answer him adequately, even if I had had the time. Despite the racist nature of the questions everyone asked, I still believed that anyone who came to a reading deserved an adequate answer, free of attack, but I did not have the time or an adequate or well thought out answer. One of the great teachers of my life was my Ta'ah, my great-grandmother. When I asked her about cannibalism, she was not offended, she simply answered: "No, or my Ta'ah would have taught me how to cook them." I decided to give the man a short response that showed intelligence because so many of the people in this room did not think I had much smarts when they came here.

Finally, after looking thoughtfully at him for a while, I said, "Thank you that you think I could," and I smiled, flashing all of my teeth. The answer shocked him as much as the question had taken me by surprise, but it made most of the men of colour in the audience chuckle. After the reading, my moderator pointed out that no white folks had laughed at my joke. Not sure why this was her first comment coming out of the reading, I responded as honestly as I could: "That's probably because they knew I was not joking," at which she laughed heartily.

We went for coffee and spent fully an hour discussing that question after the reading. Now I have the time and understanding to answer it. First, it is a complicated question. I often comment that not many Canadians know very much about us. Those that do know something about us seem to tread carefully around us. Any white person who was around in the 1940s might know about the George brothers' trial in Vernon, BC, in 1936. If they do know about the George brothers, they know we have power. Not the kind of power Canadians have but a unique brand of power. We can do things.

In Merritt, BC, there was an RCMP station. The police did something to a member of the Nlaka'pamux from Merritt. So this old woman sang all night on the hill in the back of the police station. One of the RCMP died. She went home. They sent his corpse to autopsy, and his death was inexplicable. We knew what happened: we can sing you up to wellness or sing you down to illness, even death. It is the power of our songs. We can even raise our poles with song. I should say, we could then.

The police arrested four brothers and charged them with the murder. The Nlaka'pamux protested every day of the trial, until the trial was held in secret. They hung the brothers for it, but most people knew it was that old shaman who killed the cop and they feared us. Even the RCMP feared us. One of the cops I knew from Alberta used to say: "The *see* of the Cree in Alberta is legendary. If a child got lost, the cops went to an old shaman woman. She sang a song, holding an article of clothing of the child, then told them where to look. Generally, they found her or him exactly where the old woman told them. I tell you, we had a healthy respect for that old lady. We treated her and her relations right. No telling what she could do," the RCMP said to our chief after telling him a story about her.

I talked with my friend about the fear white people have of us that drove them to believe that we really could drive them into the sea. She agreed with me. "What?" I asked, sipping my tea. "You think I could?" I should not have got as excited as I did. "Maybe not you," she said softly, "but one of your shamans could." She told me how the Mozambique Liberation Front began with a shaman singing outside the chief's post, the soldiers running out screaming and forgetting their weapons, the Mozambicans running in and stealing the soldier's weapons and bullets, then arresting the soldiers. I stared at her, a half grin on my face, and said, "You don't know that I am not a shaman's daughter." "But I do know you wouldn't, which is because your values make it impossible, in which case you can't." "That is true," I said, and we both laughed.

But I wondered still if that old man was talking about this kind of power. People whispered about us. They talked about shamanism, about devil worship, and even Voodoo. They had witnessed things. Old Dominic Charlie would get dressed in his regalia and get onstage and begin to shake. The women would sing. After a few minutes Old Dominic would burst into the air, fly six feet off the ground from a straight standing position, and then he would dance. He was well into his nineties the last time I saw him dance like that. We all stood stock-still when he did that and the white folks hissed with fear. We would later laugh.

Old Dominic was as kind as a Squamish man could be, but he was as loyal to his people as he could be too. Is that where the white man's fear emanates from? On the one hand, some of us have extraordinary powers. We are, many of us, as a result of the legacy of residential school, afraid to talk about these powers, or gifts, as the elders call them. Seattle once said, "The white man has to realize that there is more than one way of seeing." We heal ourselves through song and we can also make others sick, even die through song. We can empower ourselves through our seeing, singing, and bodywork. Many of us are fiercely loyal to ourselves. The Kwakwelth were described as completely recalcitrant and committed to their culture, stubbornly holding potlatch after it was banned, going to jail for it, but coming out and doing it all again. We were afraid to talk about this in my generation because our elders were punished severely for it. But today, everything is out in the open, the gifts are returning, and we are talking about it. Had this white man witnessed some shaman's power?

That was the public I met in the mid to late seventies. *Bobbi Lee* did well (she is still in print), and people called upon me to speak and clear up their ignorance. I struggled mightily to be as neutral about answering questions as my Ta'ah, but I did not always succeed.

Conversation 2:
Who are we separately and together?

Much of my writing has a political bent; even my poetry and novels come from my considerably long and deep past here on this continent—even when I don't intend to be political, the direction I come from makes my work *sound* political. Perhaps because of this I am sometimes invited to give keynote addresses to those who oppose the oppression of Indigenous people. Issues of poverty, water, the murdered and missing Indigenous women and girls, and the politics of colonization and decolonization often come up. The issue of Indigenous women, particularly that of the murdered and missing women and girls, comes up at almost every gathering.

This issue has become hot since the RCMP study indicated that the number of murdered women and girls exceeded the number that Indigenous women had tracked. We had thought there were over six hundred murdered or missing women and girls. The RCMP investigation, cursory as it was, doubled the number. Given the way the RCMP calculated who was missing and murdered, there are rumours the number is much higher. Consequently, I have sat on a number of panels that are directly related to the subject. I am not sure why the murder of Indigenous women is connected to identity, but it often comes up during such panels. Someone asked me if my identity was connected to resolving the crisis of Indigenous missing and murdered women. At first I stared at them, thinking, I wonder if they know how mean and thoughtless that sounds. My humanity is connected to caring for others, so is Canadian humanity, not exactly sure how that relates to identity, but I am sure I do this work because I care.

This question of identity is incredibly important to those who ask me. Some of them seem desperate to know that I have somehow hung on to my identity and get some pride from it. It is as if Canadians want to know that the oppression and domination aimed at us by Canada has not affected me much. At the same time, I wonder, like Daniel Francis maintains in *The Imaginary Indian*, whether or not the identity of Canadians is tied to the identity of Indigenous people in this country. In which case, I understand the panic. If Canadian identity is bound to Indigenous identity, any loss of identity would adversely affect Canadians—although Indigenous identity is never brought up quite that way.

On one such occasion I was asked about identity after I finished speaking about the missing and murdered women. This struck me as odd, given the subject. What also struck me as odd was that there was no question about Canadian identity. The absence of questioning Canadian identity was palpable. It seems that the identity of Canadians is unassailable. The only identity up for grabs was ours. While I processed this, I gave a nationalist answer: I am a sovereign Sto:lo woman. I answer to no man. I am not confused about my identity. In fact, I don't believe I have an identity issue. I have an issue with the sort of colonialism that still keeps the Sto:lo nation repressed. This does not mean that Sto:los do not have an identity—we do. We are aware of it and have no quandaries about it.

Canadians are who they are, and this is not a question that matters one way or another to them. It is as if it does not matter whether or not Canadians even have an identity. It is as if they do not need one. As long as we have an identity, or are solving our identity issues, Canadians will be okay. I am not quite sure how the identity of Indigenous people became fallible and questionable to Canadians, while their own identity is not, but I can say this much: I do not recall ever having doubts about my identity. The point they are making is that my identity is violable—it can be violated.

Here is my innocence: I do things much the same way my ancestors did. I learned very early that yelling in the house invites demented spirits in to drive everybody nuts, so I don't allow it and I don't do it. When someone yells, I toss them out and immediately smudge out the house. Not sure if this man asking me about identity knows about this, but it is central to who I am as a Sto:lo woman: the house is mine. I am responsible for the social relations within that house. One hundred and fifty years ago there would have been 450 people in that house that I was responsible for. I would have handled things in much the same way as I do now, through firmness, kindness, and ceremony.

I do recall in the 1970s that Canadians questioned whether they had a definable Canadian literature, which strikes me as an identity question, but it doesn't seem to strike Canadians quite the same way. In any case, the question of Canadian identity rarely comes up anymore.

Daniel Francis wrote that the question of what it is to be a Canadian is dependent on the images Canadians have of Indigenous people. *The Imaginary Indian* is a good read. I don't agree with everything Francis says, but he definitely shows the co-dependence of Canadian national selfhood or identity and the national stereotypical images Canada has of us. He also points out how false these images can be. In *The Inconvenient Indian*, Tom King shows how, after the boarding-school experience, many of us in the sixties came to rely on the generic stereotype of Indigenous people promoted by Hollywood. He offers himself and his colleagues in San Francisco as examples. True to King's form, the description of the fashion of the day for Indigenous men is quite humorous. While this is a different approach than Francis's on the issue of identity, the texts of both books rings true even today. King's take seems to spring from Francis's text on the co-dependence of Canadians on the stereotypes they developed regarding Indigenous people, even though King is referring to Americans and Native Americans. In any case, we are out of the fort, out of their story, and nowhere near their population.

On another occasion someone in the audience asked me how I felt about my identity. I answered that I had been introduced as a member of the Sto:lo nation, and no one in the Sto:lo nations had indicated any emotional identity quandaries to me and I don't have any identity issues or emotional doubts about myself, so I guess I feel all right about my identity. I made a mental note of the question this man asked. It required more thought than I could give it just then. It seemed to demand a longer answer than I initially gave him. I had a feeling it was a deeper question than I at first realized. I did mention *The Imaginary Indian*. I did not mention *The Inconvenient Indian*, as it had not been written yet.

Since Francis and King have already written on identity, I am going to come at the question from another angle. There is another serious question attached to this discussion. Who are

Canadians and Indigenous people separately and together? I once did some comedy on how Indians and tourists have a lot in common; first, to be an Indian you have to leave your village. In your village, you are a Sto:lo, or an Ojibway, a Cree, etc., but once you leave your village you become a generic Indian and that has its comic moments. I was sitting on a stone at the corner of Spadina Avenue and Bloor Street in Toronto about six or seven years ago, reading the *Metro* newspaper when two young white Canadian women came up to me and offered me some cereal. It was a brand I didn't recognize. They looked at the two Indigenous men sitting on a bench not far away and said, "Here is some more, you can share it with your friends," in that sort of enthusiastic voice kindergarten teachers use with their little charges. I was a bit confused, but it is an old Sto:lo belief that if someone offers you something, you take it. To refuse it would be to insult their offering as worthless. I presumed these two women meant well so I thanked them and left shortly after them.

When I came to work I mentioned the cereal story to my fellow colleagues. They all roared with laughter. "Lee, they thought you were homeless," they informed me. And they thought that was a riot—a famous, award-winning author accepting cereal along with the homeless Indigenous people at Bloor and Spadina. "I should buy some better clothes," I said. And they laughed some more. "Oh well, it keeps me humble," I added. Cherie Dimaline, one of my favourite young fiction writers, still finds this story funny and continues to mention it. The point is that the goodness the two women felt about giving me the cereal was not about advertising a new brand of health food by passing out boxes of the product, which is what they were hired to do, but rather it was hinged on the idea of the two women feeding someone they thought was homeless.

I was presumed homeless and hungry because I was an Indian sitting on a rock at the corner of Bloor and Spadina. Still, I ate the cereal.

A Canadian would have taken pains to explain that (she/I) was not homeless and refused the gift of cereal. Not so a Sto:lo. When a gift is offered, we graciously accept, particularly when it is food.

Canada is often referred to as multicultural, but Canadians are not multicultural. Generally, Canadians live in their little racialized neighbourhoods, interacting with their own kind. Canada cannot be multicultural if it continues to be more or less tribal, or ethnically connected to the people from which it arises. We still have "Little Italy," "Greek Villages," "Chinatown," etc., in almost every major city in Canada. Canada used to be referred to as a melting pot, but it isn't that either. Nor is it a cultural mosaic. Some people wear their cultural dress, while the majority dress in conformity with the fashion of the day, but a cultural mosaic is more than dressing like your people back home. A cultural mosaic is an agglomeration of equally recognized and utilized cultures coming together to augment the original cultural group known as Canadians. This has never happened. Canada is a British-dominated nation that diminishes all other cultures and promotes its own.

Humans are the accumulation of the cultural praxes of their forbears. Canada was once Indigenous. The very moment England and France set foot on its soil, they invoked the authority of their Crown's "right of discovery" and began changing the land and its people. While Canada is not Indigenous, it is not without Indigenous influence. The influence, however, is unknown to Canadians and unrecognized by Canada's government. Canadians believe that their cultural foundations are British.

We see Canada's cultural foundations as imperial and colonial. The Britishness of the national identity has shifted across the sands of time, but it is not viewed as eliminated. The sense of courtesy of the British aristocracy still has a strong presence in Canada, and we all are expected to adore the queen, no matter which country we are originally from. For many of us this is a painful colonial expectation, but no matter, we must love the queen. Canadians also have this identity of niceness or kindness that is fallacious as well. Thousands of immigrants are called to Canada every year, the processing of their education credentials happens at a snail's pace, and the newcomers are often forced to work two jobs at significantly lower pay than their professional credentials would entitle them, just to make ends meet while they wait for the processing of the proper documents that would allow them to work at their profession. This is a national scandal and has surfaced a number of times in various newspapers. The last article on it that I read talked about a professor working at two jobs as a cleaner. She sent her child to school with only one apple as his fruit of the day. The newspaper asked why this was happening in one of the richest countries in the world. Colonialism is my answer. Say this to Canadians and they will look aghast and say they did not know. The articles were written in English in the same newspapers that are published daily in Canada, yet they claimed not to know. Denial. To be a white Canadian is to be sunk in deep denial.

Indigenous concepts of family were altered more than a century ago, very violently. While my grandfather was at school, they burned all of the longhouses of his village and told people to build homes like white men. The people of my grandfather's village did. He returned confused about where his village was. The landscape looked right but the houses did not. He feared that his family had been removed. He wandered up and down the length of the inlet until finally, his mother found him wandering back and forth across his ancestral village. We were not nuclear-family-oriented, but once the longhouses were burned and we were forced into single-family units, we began to change the way we interacted with one another.

Indigenous concepts of citizenship are absent. Canadian concepts were imposed on us: first, through the restrictions placed upon physical movement, and second, through legislative acts regarding Indians. Along with the insistence on nuclear-family living arrangements came male lineage and the insistence on a woman moving to a man's village upon marriage. In the Indian Act, Indigenous people were legally deemed unfit to govern and to vote, as they were considered children in the eyes of the law. Women once carried the bundle of keeping the backward and forward vision of the nation and transmitting the culture. They carried bundles of management, social organization, and economic distribution that have now become concepts hanging loose between time and space. The birthright of our women has been curtailed, restricted, and violated. We have become inferior beings in the eyes of the citizens of Canada and of many of the men in our own homes. The actual place of women does not change, whether or not we were intended to occupy the original space and exercise power. That we no longer have this place does not eradicate it, it just means that colonial authority still has us in its grip. To some degree, we accept its authority over the authority of Indigenous women.

British colonialism began as a benefit to white British men. They got ahead, fixed the laws and policies for newcomers so that they would always be ahead. Every year Statistics Canada prints statistics comparing the income of women against the income of men. In 2011, women made 87 cents on the man's dollar. That year, Indigenous educated women with post-secondary degrees made more than white educated women with a similar level of education: the median income of Indigenous women with a university degree was $49,947; the median income of white women with a university degree was $47,742. That was the year Harper dropped the penny. I swore at a number of gatherings that he did that on purpose. The issue of equal pay for work of equal value hasn't budged much for women—white men are still way ahead. This is also true for men of colour in relation to women of color, but those statistics are apparently harder to calculate.

And yet I have heard the deputy minister of immigration for Canada urge newcomers gaining citizenship to forget their country of origin. Until there is economic or financial fairness or equality between white men and the rest of us, the pot is not melting: it is boiling over with segregation and cultural dismissal of others. There is no mosaic, and there is clearly economic segregation. And asking the newcomers to forget any aspect of their previous nation means they cannot make a cultural contribution to the mosaic. Worse, it means their contribution is worthless to those who have established cultural, racial, and gender superiority. The multicultural nature of the country becomes washed out as newcomers continue to arrive.

Education is a cultural process and, of course, the education citizens receive in Canada is all about British contact with Indigenous people and the development and maintenance of Canada. No one studies what was here before in any serious way. It is as though the 150-year history of Canada is far more significant than the 15,000 years previous. Even then it is a distorted history of such important people as John A.

MacDonald, the first prime minister, and his great vision of a railroad uniting the country. My favourite poem, "Letter to Sir John A. Macdonald," is a "Dear John letter" written by Marilyn Dumont and published in her fine book *A Really Good Brown Girl*; in this poem she talks to Sir John and reminds him she is still here and half-breed, and—funny thing—he is gone.

Very little of the education offered by Canadian schools is about the building of the railroad by Indigenous and Chinese labourers, many of whom went unpaid and most of whom never received their pensions. The word *shanghaied* comes from the press gangs that kidnapped the men of Shanghai and brought them to Canada to work on the railroads. Their women were not allowed to come with them, so some took Indigenous wives, particularly in BC. China Bar Tunnel is named after the dead Chinese men buried there in the stone and rock after they were killed instead of paid. This multicultural fact remains unknown by most people in this country. Instead we are taught that MacDonald built the railroad.

The railroad's construction was opposed by Indigenous people in northeastern Ontario who supported Louis Riel's vision of Manitoba, and very little is taught about that either. We are told about the Underground Railroad to Canada for fleeing black slaves, as though Canada were already a land of freedom, but we are not told that the United Empire Loyalists were permitted to keep their slaves, until the Loyalist's death, even though slavery was outlawed in Canada. Nova Scotia's Black township in Halifax purchased by Black Canadians and destroyed by white Canadians is not spoken of, and of course the constant death of Indigenous people, the headhunting of the Beothuk of Newfoundland, etc., is not taught.

Further, Canadians are taught that they came here to save

us. I have been told occasionally that we should be grateful. Some Canadians have a difficult time when we are doing well because of this notion that they are here to help us. They almost seem happy when we are *not* doing well, and of course Canada makes sure we do not do better than the majority of Canadians.

When the British first came, chronic cultural collision occurred between the newcomers and the original inhabitants, but the concept of cultural collision is never discussed in our schools or elsewhere. When Europeans first came, washing the body naked was a dirty, filthy sin against god. No one stripped naked in England to wash. Public bathing occurred once a year in town fountains. Garbage was thrown out the windows into the gutters, along with feces, urine, and dead babies. The conditions were so awful that Dryden felt compelled to write a poem about it. This is often referred to as the first environmental poem. Toronto covered its rivers in the mid-1700s to stem the tide of cholera and typhus epidemics that killed so many of its citizens. Cholera and typhus are diseases caused by filth. It was not until the late 1800s that doctors were compelled to wash their hands when working from patient to patient. Before that, thousands of women died during childbirth. But it was Indigenous people who were referred to as filthy savages precisely *because* they stripped naked and washed every day. Washing of the hands is still difficult to enforce in modern hospitals, as drug-resistant bacterial infection increases and steals the lives of many patients after surgery.

From the early 17ᵗʰ century to the late 19ᵗʰ century generally and until the 1920s in areas of the north where there were no hospitals, many white women preferred Indigenous midwives to physicians, who led the banning of midwives and conducted a devastating ideological campaign against natural medicine that continues to this day. Witchcraft, old wives' tales, and so forth demean our medical knowledge. Cultural knowledge of Indigenous people was suppressed by Canada until recently, and Canadians, for the most part, went along with their government. Because the economy of Canada continued to improve with the deepening of the exploitation of Indigenous lands, there was a certain amount of faith in and acceptance of the inevitability of Canadian citizens exploiting Indigenous lands. White men were granted land for very little money and sometimes the land grants were free, while Indigenous people were confined to small reserves and in some provinces not allowed to purchase land.

Education became the key to growing economic power in the country. Literacy is now one of the international yardsticks the colonizer and former colonizers use to determine progress. Eventually, education was made compulsory for all Canadians, including Indigenous people. Until the sixties, education in Canada—particularly English education—was heavy-handedly British. Corporal punishment was used in most school districts until it was banned in the sixties. In BC, it took the death of a hemophiliac at my school to end the striking of a student by a teacher. Eventually, the strap was banned. In the high school I went to, brawls between students and teachers were commonplace. Education was about promoting whiteness and maleness. While women were not officially barred from attending university, few were accepted. In 1972 my sister was not allowed to take an electrical course because she was a female. So white guys got ahead, and now they tell us to pull up our socks and work hard.

Segregation was common in Canada and the United States. The dates of legal segregation vary with provincial and state law, but the pass system so infamous in South Africa has its origins in Canada. One such segregation by-law in North Vancouver affected my family. The by-law forbade any "Indians, Jews, Blacks or Asians" from living in Lynn Valley, where my mother had purchased a home. The law was still on the books when we moved there, and the community tried to petition the city to get us evicted. While the attempt failed, the law remained on the books.

For Canada to suddenly declare itself a multicultural country without evidence or praxis was farcical. Many people of color rallied and challenged and continue to challenge the so-called multicultural nature of Canada. Canada set up a multicultural funding program, but much of the monies went to white, non-English Canadians. Being Canadian was about jilting people of color out of whatever funds were available in the arts and cultural life of the country for a long time and maintaining strict denial of the racist and colonial nature of Canada. In fact, Canadians often ask me, "But isn't it better in Canada than in the United States?" That is a mountain of denial. How can one colonial system be better than another?

"But aren't Indians about sharing?" some well-meaning Canadian says from the audience when I talk about returning lands. Canada recently made some comment about how we are doing much better by not having economic equality with Canadians.

When I first began writing, many people asked me to come and "educate" their groups and I would ask for an honorarium. For a long time, people would respond to my request, "Aren't Indians about sharing?" Yes, well, we already gave, and look where that got us—you took the whole continent. I explained that sharing is when I give you something and you give me something. I give you an education and you pay for it; that is the sort of sharing I will participate in, and I would remind you that slavery is outlawed in this country. This kind of question went on until the nineties, when people began to realize we had some self-respect.

When Europeans first came to North America, Indigenous people agreed to let them build a house and access the land so they could feed themselves in the way we did. At the time, we had unrestricted access to every square inch of North America, and Europeans had access to those lands we permitted them to use. We did not agree that Europeans should then give this country to their monarchs to own and exploit forever and all time. Nor did we agree that the monarchs should then dominate us and dictate what we can and cannot do.

It was easy to avoid conquest in the beginning, but as more and more people made their way here, and more and more of us died of European disease, it became impossible to fend off domination. Laws were made to restrict our movement, even to prevent us from ever becoming legal adults or citizens. Until we became citizens in 1962 we came under immigration law as permanent foreigners unless we disenfranchised ourselves, and some of us did just that. Most of us simply suffered in horrific silence.

In Canadian people's defense, they claim not to know what was going on. Well, everyone knew that Indigenous people came from here and non-Indigenous people came from somewhere else. No one became curious about how the shift from Indigenous authority over the land to Canadian authority over the land occurred, nor did they become curious about how our access to the land and its wealth became restricted. No one became curious about how Canadian law became the law that dominated the entire landscape. No one got curious about what was here before. History has been taught from Europe's point of view, and Canadian history begins with colonization by Britain, which led to Confederation. It seems Indigenous people were passive bystanders, nearly invisible in the historic alteration of the landscape and the development of the power relations here.

Conversation 3:
Marginalization and reactionary politics

I began coming to Ontario in the mid-1980s, around the time of the early dub poets. I had been reading poetry in Vancouver for some time and a group of us formed a band comprised of my very young teenage daughters and a fellow college student—Russell Wallace, who was even then magic on his keyboards. My daughters sang backup in Ojibway or Cree and I read poetry while Russell jammed on his keyboard and the girls played the big drum. My daughters were the first all-women's big group in the country. Generally, women are *not allowed* to play the big drum. The man who taught them to drum and sing paid no attention to those rules, which he figured were patriarchal and invasive. We were generally paid by people who wanted a poem about something. I would write a poem and my band would conjure the backup song and music to go with it. It was called dub poetry, as it began with a poem and the music was dubbed in afterward.

At first there was a great deal of resistance to having Indigenous people onstage at traditional Euro-gatherings, even when plenty of other people of colour were represented.

Our music was referred to as lexically running meaningless vocables. My poetry was often dismissed as protest poetry, and people would sometimes ask me about writing protest poetry. My answer was that the term was coined to dismiss the work of Indigenous and Black dub and hip-hop poetry, so I pay no attention to such questions. I write the way I write because it is the way I think and feel about the world; the imagery is comprised of the way I see the world. I am not a fan of Yeats, who wrote that "the centre cannot hold," as though his country were the centre of the universe, but I respect that that is how he saw the position of his people in the world.

Finally, the Vancouver Folk Music Festival accepted dub poetry as folk music. Fellow dub poet Lillian Allen and our little group were invited to the festival, along with some American Indigenous bands as well. I believe dub poetry changed the way many Canadians see us. The highlight of all this performing was playing at the Vancouver Folk Music Festival and being the only group to receive a standing ovation.

My daughters were the singers, and the techies began setting up microphones for them: "No mics," we all said. The techies insisted on it. The girls began to sing. You could hear them throughout the festival, and as people began to leave the venues, they were apt to come to where the girls were singing and Russell was playing the keyboards. The techies panicked and immediately pulled the plug on the girls' microphones. But we just laughed and got on with the show. Most of our new audience members stayed to hear, and I am still proud of our standing ovation.

I left the dub poetry movement not because I did not love it—I did, but I found it difficult to memorize the lines of my own poetry. Onstage with such icons as Lillian Allen, who recited her work from heart, I looked a little ridiculous to myself. No one else but me seemed to mind it. Besides, my daughters went off to theatre school and so I lost my backup. People did invite me to read poetry without the musical backup, however, and I became comfortable doing that. My daughter Columpa and I occasionally do poetry and song together like the old days, and you can hear us on YouTube. I also preferred to include questions and answers as part of the performance. I do so enjoy interacting with the audience, even when some audience members agitate me.

I have always believed that poetry is an oral word art form, so I never tried to get it published much. This strikes me as odd now. I left the oral word art movement of dub poetry to read poetry and yet I hesitated to publish it, but there you go. I am a little quirky. Finally, Greg Younging of Theytus Books asked to publish my poetry. *Bent Box* came out of that in 2000—not a rip-roaring best seller, but it is now out of print. Theytus is not anxious to reprint it, and I am okay with that. These days, authors who can't find someone to reprint a work can always create their own e-book. If I ever find some time on my hands, I may do just that. My novels *Ravensong* and *Bobbi Lee* are back in print.

For me, performance art and storytelling are the same thing. I love getting up there and kicking it onstage, though not as a storyteller. But I seldom miss an opportunity to tell a story—I rarely do just storytelling as a rule. Dr. Dawn Maracle, during her graduate student years, outed me as a storyteller by putting me on a program at the Whetung Ojibwa Centre in Peterborough many years ago. Shannon Thunderbird was going to be there as well. She was an exceptional storyteller, and I was sharing the stage with her. I confess, I am competitive, so I stepped up my game and performed a story for no particular reason but to tell the story and entertain everyone there. There is no best storyteller award, so it did not do any good, but it made me realize I could do a good showing as a teller if all else failed.

As a thinker, an orator, and a Sto:lo, I did what other Indigenous speakers do. I blended theory and story together. I was brought up in story. No one disciplined me by spanking or scoldings; rather, the old people watching me told me a story and I was expected to figure out my behavioural issues from the story. I recall being on the platform with my ex-husband Raymond Bobb, and someone said something not too clever, and he said, "Remember, Grade 1: Think and Do." I chuckled to myself because I remember being taught that lesson when I was three years old. My caregiver asked me, "Why did you do this?" I answered, "I don't know." I no longer recall what I did, but I clearly remember being stared at. Note to self: there is no such thing as "I don't know" in my world.

Just as I was raised on story, I brought my children up on story. We work with story. We begin with an old tale and, as we progress through the story, we tell it back different but the same, changing it so it becomes a modern new story. Fiction, created as a continuum of original story. All through the days of public school, day school, and residential school, our youth did not have the opportunity to play with our own story. Canadians play with their story from the beginning of kindergarten until the end of their doctoral years. No wonder we are having a hard time—we have much to protest.

I am an orator. Salish oratory is about thinking, and the story is there to remind us or key up our thoughts. Stories are keys to the national treasure known as our knowledge. Our orators are trained to share this knowledge and give the keys to help the listener key up the knowledge when they need it—this way we don't have to memorize either the story or the knowledge. Each is the key to the other: the story reminds us of the oratory, and the oratory reminds us of the story. This is not to say we did not have story-performing artists a long time ago—we did. Those story performers were dancers, mask dancers, theatrical comics, clowns. They more properly belonged to the world of dance and theatre than to story creation, but I would not have been one of them—I would have been what I am now: an orator. I have done a great deal of performance art, but do not consider myself a performing artist—I am an orator and a writer, who does some performance.

I would not have been a storyteller because this is not what I wanted to do with story. I use story in the context of a talk to illustrate my point. I am much too political to just tell stories. In any case, it was always a struggle to get up onstage alongside white folks. In fact, the first time I read at the Vancouver Writers Festival, I crashed the stage. I had help, from my old friend Cam Hubert (commonly known as author Anne Cameron), who colluded with me, and people were shocked. The next year I came to the festival by invitation.

Not long ago I was invited again to the festival, and the person in charge of my reading reminded me of the first time I had come and crashed it. That had definitely been a protest action. Up until that point, no Indigenous writer had graced the Vancouver Writers Festival stage. After that, things changed.

During this time I met a number of Canadians who became strong allies in getting Indigenous people recognized and ensuring they had room on the stage, not the least of which was the executive director of the Vancouver Writer's Festival, Alma Lee. I recall mumbling about how I hate this continuous fighting we have to do for every little thing. I was at home in Sardis. I recall my life partner staring at me, eyebrows raised in that doubting way. "I trust you will rethink what you just said," noted my partner. I did.

"Actually, I didn't hate the fight," I said out loud. "I just hate continuously losing."

My whole family laughed.

I wrote *I Am Woman* in January 1988; Carolyn Jerome, a friend of mine who calls herself CJ, gave me the space at her house to write undisturbed for two weeks. I literally grabbed all the bits of paper I had in an old box and conjured the book. The Women of Color Press in New York invited me to submit a manuscript, and I sent them *I Am Woman*. They sent me back a letter saying, among other things, that it was *too beautiful to publish as non-fiction; we would not know how to market it.* I loved that critical assessment. However you look at it, they turned the book down because it was too beautiful. It made me realize that people of colour, when they become writers and publishers, often capitulate to white male standards. I decided not to capitulate.

I Am Woman was published in 1988 by Write-On Press, and is still being reissued. It was recently longlisted by CBC's Canada Reads, the broadcaster's way of promoting literary works in Canada. This is quite the feat for a book that is thirty-nine years old.

At the 1988 Feminist Book Fair in Montreal I asked the feminists to "move over." Indigenous women took the event by storm. They were by far the best-selling writers, their performances the most attended. It was as though the feminists had woken up and turned around, as Black American feminists had instructed them to do, and then they saw us standing there. This did not mean they were no longer racist, as the organizers mistreated the Black feminist authors of Montreal, but we were able to run interference with the organizers and bring them in line. You do not invite people to participate after you have organized the conference for them (paternalism) and selected the authors who would attend: "Nothing about us without us," lesbian women in Vancouver shouted out a few years back to feminists who were trying to organize on their behalf. Still, quite a number of publishers after that were interested in our work, including a Toronto-based small press called Sister Vision, where another feminist author published a collection of Indigenous women's poetry. Connie Fife, the editor, has since passed into the spirit world, but like a good Indigenous woman, she gave a number of Indigenous lesbian and women authors a leg up.

It seems that Euro-academics cannot handle being fair to all of us at the same time. Rumour has it that at the recent TransCanadas 2017 conference, Black academics complained about being tokens. They did not complain about us being featured, but I felt embarrassed that we were featured while Blacks were ignored. I am aware, however, that if Blacks are featured, we and the Asians are often left out, and so forth. We need to be able to handle all of us together. We also need to support each other. Few people of colour attend Indigenous gatherings and few Indigenous people attend people-of-colour gatherings. The gossamer-thin walls need to come down, painful as that may be. Maybe it will be the young hip-hop artists who bring them down and stop holding up the binary of race.

Some Canadian recently asked me what I thought of Black Lives Matter. And I wanted to be snippy and say, "Why, don't you agree that black lives matter?" But that was not what the Canadian was trying to do. It seems that since Trump was elected, Black people sticking up for themselves has become tantamount to racism. That would make Dr. King a big racist; it would make Rosa Parks a racist. I am with Malcolm X on this one: that is the thief blaming the victim. Black Lives Matter has gotten a bad rap in the press. They are called racist for advocating for Black lives. That is such a misuse of the word *racist*. It is not racist to defend a group people who are persecuted for their race. This particular Canadian may have been hoping to drive a wedge between us and them. I don't know, but this is how I answered:

"I like Black Lives Matter and Black Lives Matter Toronto. First, because they support Indigenous peoples' struggles. Second, because there is a great deal of racism in policing. The press keeps saying that BLMTO are preventing the police from participating in Toronto Pride. That is a lie. Yes they are, but they no longer have the privilege of having a float and having the public adore them for their participation. Securing a float is an earned privilege. Shooting Black people makes it difficult to justify giving police this privilege." I hope this answer is amenable to BLM, who I feel obligated to support because they also advocate for other people of colour and for Indigenous people and because someone has to face the fact that Black lives don't count for enough in this country—they do matter.

Today I am adding this: Toronto Chief of Police Mark Saunders made it plain that he will not come without the privilege. This makes previous police participation disingenuous. Give us a special place and we will come. I have been attending Pride for over a decade and a half, with no hope of any privilege and no attempt at receiving it. I have read every article on it, and at no time does the chief (who happens to be Black) say, "Okay, let's talk about straightening out police relations with Blacks and men of colour," nor has he pledged to stop shooting Black men or men of colour. By the way, Canadians are not talking much about the foregoing either. Like BLM, I will not be marginalized. We Matter. Reactionary politics for Canadians, and protest politics for us. So here it is: good for Pride: the police do not deserve a float. Earn it.

One Canadian woman once asked me if it was a contradiction being an Indigenous woman and a feminist. This is a convoluted question. First, it says that patriarchy either a) has no effect on us, or b) we like it, or c) it runs contrary to our culture or, as some people say, is a foreign concept. I dismiss the last point: many English concepts are foreign. We cannot help that: patriarchy, racism, homophobia, transgendered dismissal, invisibility and dismissal and sexism are all foreign. Colonialism is foreign. Clear-cutting is foreign, and so forth. But the only time Canadians pick up on the foreignness of a concept to our culture is when it has to do with women. Some of our own people have picked different sides of the not allowed because it is a foreign argument line around feminism, including women. Some women maintain that we are not feminists because we are *gender complementary*, that is a system which had a male and a female heads of governance. Our societies of the past were gender-complementary societies. Some even hold that they were matriarchal, but they are not that now. Restoring our world to gender-complementary societies is a feminist act. Our societies were also independent societies with unlimited access to the wealth of the land. The Sto:lo were foreigners to the Kwakwelth and the Haida people. So we are accustomed to dealing with foreigners. No one suggested we could not have something foreign; in fact, we traded with each other for foreign goods. This has nothing to do with how we organize our societies. Patriarchy is a systemic invasion and must be repelled as unjust, not because it is foreign but because it is mean.

On another occasion an elder white Canadian asked, "But

isn't feminism foreign?" I wanted to say, "First, we are as entitled to foreign things as anyone in the world," but I didn't say that. Instead, I answered, "Not as foreign as capitalism and colonialism," to much laughter from the audience. His response was "But don't you think—" I cut him off mid-sentence with "All the time. I think all the time." This generated more laughter. I was wary of a loaded questioned preceded by *Don't you think...?* This question was advanced by a white man. If you disagree, you are ipso facto not thinking—as though white men were the arbiters of what is thinking and what is not. After saying I think all the time, I just looked at him—with that Sto:lo gramma stare that can fry your insides. That is patriarchy for you.

Now some of our own people are repeating the phrase: "Feminism comes from the outside." I want to say, "So do Levi's," but I bite my tongue and opt for reason. I get why men are doing it. Having only one chief is handy. Not having to deal with women leaders is handy. Actually, it is patriarchy that comes from outside, and feminism is its most effective response. Far from being foreign, feminism is homegrown as a result of the relationship between a Seneca woman and Elizabeth Cady Stanton.

A Seneca woman inspired Elizabeth to launch the suffragettes. Elizabeth was a friend of the now-Shenandoahs from New York. She came over to visit her Seneca woman friend one day. Her friend told her that she was going to buy the white man's farm that just went up for sale. "What does your husband say about that?" Elizabeth asked. "Nothing," her friend answered. "I am buying it, not him." Elizabeth scoffed, "You can't buy a farm without his permission, and you are a woman." Her friend laughed and said, "No, you can't buy a farm without your husband's permission, and you are a white woman.

See all that land out there: it is mine." First Elizabeth had to learn about Six Nations sovereignty. How could these people have different laws? Then Elizabeth and her friend sat down and Elizabeth learned about the matriarchal governance of the Six Nations Confederacy. It was from that foundation that feminism and the suffragette movement was born. It is not a bit foreign. It is rooted in the Haudenosaunee system. There is a book out there thanking the Shenandoah family. It is no more foreign than many of the concepts Europeans borrowed from us, like cleanliness, democracy, and kindness to children.

"Push comes to shove," someone once said, "you get rid of patriarchy and I will stop being a feminist." I am not sure I would stop being a feminist. There is always a danger of returning to the same old despotic ways.

All of the above is connected to the continuous attempt by Canada and Canadians to marginalize us from inside our nations. To say feminism is foreign suggests we do not belong in the centre of feminist politics. We do. The foregoing statements are lame attempts to consign us to a place on the edges of our nations, just outside the fort—an attempt to segregate and oppress us.

Even when we were confined to spaces outside the fort, we were never on capitalism's margin. Our wealth is the engine that keeps Canadian settlers privileged. Their failure to share what they have stolen makes us look as though we are on the margins, but without our wealth, Europeans would become the impoverished souls who arrived here four centuries ago. Colonialism is the centre of the capitalist economy. It is the foundations of capitalist imperialism, and we will not be marginalized inside our nations.

The beatings Indigenous people at Standing Rock continuously received over the pipeline under Obama's leadership show how central the natural-resource wealth of our lands is to the larger society. Tar sands and Kinder Morgan are the Canadian equivalent. The attack by police against the Mi'kmaq people protesting fracking on October 18, 2013 is but another example of how desperately Canada needs our wealth. We are not permitted to protest, and this makes it look like we are on the margin, but the reason we are not permitted to protest is that the resources (oil in particular) are critical to the maintenance of Canadian privilege and that puts us in the center of progressive politics, and in the centre of the economy.

The notion of marginalization is conjured by those who believe we want to be a part of this racist, colonial, patriarchal world that is struggling to maintain its grip on our continent and on the former colonies, particularly Africa. It looks as though Indigenous people are all saying, "What about me, pick me, take me." I feel more like Leanne Betasamosake Simpson, Cherie Dimaline, Marilyn Dumont, Greg Schofield, Maria Campbell, Tom King, and Jeannette Armstrong, who are interested in continuing the work of the foremothers and forefathers, who have never felt they were on anyone else's margin, but have always been central to their own world.

Some of the Canadians who genuinely care about us but cannot conceive of not being the center of the universe refer to us as Canada's national tragedy. To believe that everyone wants to be you is psychotic at worst and deluded at best. I wrote *Talking to the Diaspora* as a response to the notion of environmental permission to exploit whatever resource humans want to exploit. My poem "Blind Justice," in that collection, was a response to marginalization on the edges of Canada, as though this fit Canadians' notion of us being a national tragedy, Canada's tragedy. You don't own us. You never owned us. We own ourselves. Get used to it.

Conversation 4:
What can we do to help?

Almost every time I give a reading or a talk, someone will ask, "What can we do to help?" After presenting on all of the injustices in Canada when it comes to Indigenous people, I almost want to laugh and ask just exactly what they would like to help with—Canada does quite well as a colonizer.

Instead, while performing at the museum for Article 11 in the show *Ask an Elder*, I said something like: "Why, do I look fragile to you?" I wanted to answer, "I would like to live among thinking, non-racist human beings—can you make that happen? I could use a little help here." The question "What can we do to help?" implies that we are responsible for achieving some monumental task we are not up to and so the offer of help is generous. It infers that we had some hand in how things turned out for us. Racism and colonialism and patriarchy are Canadian social formations, not Indigenous ones. We are not the only ones responsible for their undoing. If you participate in dismantling the master's house and ending all forms of oppression, you are helping yourself. The sooner Canadians realize that, the better. Elijah Harper, in a speech at the Stein

Valley Festival in 1990, said, "Whenever Indigenous people achieve reform or end an injustice, you benefit."

In fact, it is Canadians who need help in realizing that the nature of their society is not of our making and that their acceptance of it taints their national character and their country. It is their responsibility to change their society, which is racist, colonial, and patriarchal to the core. During the Oka Crisis of 1990, the Ku Klux Klan held a gathering on a farm in southern Alberta. A group of grey-haired white women went onto the farm with their mops and brooms to clean things up. "Get out of here. We will have no more of this," they said as they chased the Klan into their cars and sent them packing. They were helping themselves to a better country.

In line with having no clue about their world, Canadians continue to insist that they are "better than America." There is the myth of the nice Canadians, the just society; meanwhile, underneath is all this falsehood. England colonized both America and Canada, then relinquished its hold on both of them at different points in history, but the foundations of the colonial relations were established by Britain: racism, slavery, colonialism, and patriarchy. And there has been no successful revolution to alter that. The difference between the United States and Canada is that Native Americans of the U.S. have much bigger reservations than do we.

By better, I presume Canadians mean they are nicer than Americans—Canadians have a reputation for that. In fact, Americans always say, "If you step on a Canadian's foot, the Canadian will apologize." I would add: until they notice the colour of the person who owns the foot, then they are just as likely to stare at you for standing under their feet. Native American reserves are on average three hundred times larger than Canadian reserves. We were confined to treaty territories with reserves inside them. Americans were given reservations that covered the entire treaty territory. The problem for all Indigenous Turtle Islanders is that the state—Canada and America—determines what we are entitled to within our territories. What is better—not allowed or Not Allowed? I leave it to Canadians to decide.

Someone once said that Canadians are happiest when we are doing poorly. I don't mean to ally with cynicism, but sometimes I think some Canadians believe that if we begin to do better, this makes them lesser people. Some Canadians believe we will want to be Canadians. Our standard of life overall has not improved greatly, but we have begun to see economic differences between us. This is not necessarily a good thing, but it shows that the economy is not in our hands. We have little control over it. Linda Tuhiwai Smith warned us in a talk she gave at the University of Toronto to First Nations people: "We should be careful what we ask for, because they can give it to us." There is some truth in that. The working class in this country asked for higher wages during the prosperous fifties, and they got it at the expense of Africa and Southern Asia. The money has to come from somewhere, and it isn't going to be from the one per centers.

In *Soul on Ice*, Eldridge Cleaver called oppression in America oppression between silk sheets. This surprised me, as not even the paid leaders could afford silk sheets at the time. (That is not the case today. Phil Fontaine made sure that the grand chief receives a tax-free salary of $120,000 a year.) In the sixties, Indigenous people received much less pay for the same work as their white counterparts.

But no matter how much money you give me, it is not the same as sovereignty and the right to caretake our lands. Many of us understand this. It is imperative to say no to earth rape:

no to Kinder Morgan is worth all the money you can muster. We are not afraid of hardship.

I once heard Leanne Betasamosake Simpson talk about being a "recovering academic." I found this so funny, and laughed out loud when she said it. I looked around but no one else was laughing. Apparently, Canadians love their academics and love being one. It confused the Canadians in the audience that Leanne thought academia was a sickness one had to recover from.

I apparently was the only one who agreed with her. I am not actually an academic—so I don't have to recover from that, but I am around academics all the time, and I get the humour in that remark: most of the time academics struggle to understand the jargon of their discipline, which is often Greek or Latin in origin. Since few of us speak Latin or Greek, mastering academic language is difficult for most of us. As we are being judged by our various PhD committees, we often here the judges say, "It needs more academic language," or more Greek or Latin jargon. It does not get by me that this is a fundamental insult to First Nations people.

First, Indigenous people are entitled to learn from within our cultures. That means if a language is to be privileged, it ought to be one of ours. In the Accord on Indigenous Education, the Association of Canadian Deans of Education advocates that Indigenous people are entitled to learn from within their cultures, but professors don't often support this position. Second, it implies that the jargon is superior to whatever other languages we use. Academics struggle with it because they do not learn the language from which the jargon originates. They just learn the weak and multisyllabic terms that are rarely rooted in the English language. In other words, they are speaking a language completely bereft of story and the culture of the jargon's origin.

Imagine how meaningless that is as a process of thought and expression. It is completely spiritless and emotionless. There is nothing in your own text to ease you into your thoughts; there is no spirit-to-spirit logic to provide you with emotional guidance. Many people, such as Leanne, express their feelings of oppression as they complete their degrees. After a while nothing strikes you. Your ability to remember feels like it is drying up and your nerves begin to shatter—or at least that is how many professors start to look and behave. After a while, they seem to become the sort of academic they loathed as a student. So why do we do this to ourselves? Why don't we use the deans' commitment to our learning through our own cultures?

I went to school for some twenty years. What saved me was what my uncle says; I became "what we were and will always want to be"—which in my case was an orator. Make no mistake, I was trained to be an orator. My children are trained to speak and I make sure my current university students can get up and speak. In fact, when another professor told one of my students that he was a good speaker, he answered her by saying, "You do know Lee Maracle is my teacher." He left it that.

We have so many great speakers among us now and with a little effort we could study ourselves.

I have had the great privilege of hearing and coming to know a number of such exceptional Indigenous people. One person is the late Dr. Trish Monture. I am so sad for our youth today who will never get to hear her in person, but if anyone has a tape of her we should establish an oratorical library in her name: The Trish Monture Oratorical Library—online.

You can make it a reconciliation project. First, it would end the absurd privileging of oratory over literature, as many learned folks still say that oratory is impossible to study for the very reason of its oral nature. Technology now allows us to record and film oratory and to create the natural setting for story work. We do not, as a rule, download story, we work with story. Today, our young filmmakers are using technology to recreate the conditions for working with story on film. Many schools study *Bobbi Lee*. Not many realize it was an oral project—that it was tape recorded, transcribed, and edited. I began orating it at twenty-two years old. *Bobbi* began in a class I took, learning to do oral histories. My idea was to do oral histories with those elders who did not attend residential school.

(That would be a great project for a Canadian group to engage in, elevating oratory to the position of the written word. Oratory and literature is all word art to me. However, that is not likely a Canadian idea that would come up. They all treasure writing over oratory. We are not equal in any way in Canada's mind.)

Anyway, on this one occasion Trish gets up and starts talking: "You know the white man is emotionally stunted and spiritually crippled and he has no idea that he got that way by thingifying everything and then giving it a high highfalutin name so that we would all try to speak just like him, which we did, and now we have these institutions full of empty, uncaring academics who speak a crazy combination of culturally disconnected jargon made of Greek, English, and Latin, and are completely not understandable; all the while they maintain that this business of thingifying is the gold standard of all speaking, thinking, and knowing—and yes, I am aware that this past thought is framed in a long-ass run-on sentence, thank you very much. Consequently, we know nothing and nothing changes."

This brings me to the myth of academia and objectivity. Or as Trish would put it: thingifying everything. Objectivity is a ruse we pass on to young students and we use it to close the gates to those who have little or no faith in capitalism. I was taught that Neanderthals originated in Africa, travelled to Europe, and became extinct because they were not as bright as the more modern European humans. This was considered a scientific fact. Today, it appears that the Neanderthals were from Europe. And lo and behold, they weren't so stupid after all. There is little objectivity, even in the hard sciences.

We should all be studying Trish Monture and examining the myth of objectivity. I am not as quick to dismiss it as Trish, but I do know that it is a myth. I also know there are elements of truth in mythology, and they should not be dismissed. During the 1993 crisis in Navajo territory with Hantavirus, a group of scientists were trying to figure out where the disease was coming from so they could test it. A young Navajo asked an elder lady, and she told him the story of how the mouse and the humans were not supposed to live in the same house. It took the scientists a while to figure out she was giving them the culprit to test. It turned out to be true. The mouse carried the disease and passed it on to humans. Kill the mice, evict them from the homes, and eradicate the disease.

I also know the concept of zero and subtraction is a myth too, but the world has reinvented itself over and over through its various mythologies. Almost all so-called human progress is connected to our mythologies either directly or indirectly. Where we get ourselves in trouble is when we declare by dint of the bayonet that one set of mythologies is based on science proper and all other mythologies are balderdash. There is something useful in every story.

It is complicated, but I hope you find it interesting enough to follow along and examine this with me.

Someone asked me once about the value of myth to any given society. Well, we do not have to dig too deep to see the value of the myth Cinderella to capitalist/monarchist patriarchy—just read the *Cinderella Complex*. Patriarchy is our social order, and retelling the Cinderella story and the variations on it ensures its continuance by securing the cooperation of all the little Cinderellas to come. "Why can't your daughters forget Cinderella and fight for equal pay for equal work?" Your daughters cannot fight something as innocuous as Cinderella, but we are expected to just forget 150 years of continuous horror and move along. Not only that, but Canada is asking us to give up our fundamental myths that are thousands and thousands of years old.

Women need to hold up patriarchy in order for patriarchy to remain unchanged. This is how it works: 70 per cent of all books sold are purchased by women and 80 per cent of those books are written by men: we are purchasing the books holding up patriarchy. So when Canadians ask us, "Why can't you just forget what happened and join our society?" you need to look in the mirror and examine yourself—forget about math, stop developing technology, buildings, etc., including nuclear technology, and rein in the production of plastics.

Non-Indigenous women need to be complacent for Canada and Canadians to get away with killing Indigenous women with impunity. Feminism is for all women. Equality is for all humans.

Once an audience member said, "Why can't Indigenous people grasp math? Is it because they cannot engage in abstract thought?" I wanted to answer, "We can engage in abstract thought—we have been engaging your government in justice negotiations, which is very abstract to capitalism and its supporters of colonialism. In any case, your government cannot grasp it. It just depends what thought you are abstracting from the normal beliefs." I didn't say that. Instead, I told this story.

And what about math? In Grade 2 my teacher was trying to teach me subtraction and so she took six beans in her hand and held them out for me to see: "How many beans?" I answer, "Six." She removes two and hides them behind her back: "Now how many?" "You still have six—you are just hiding two." This sort of pragmatic logic is what got us called incapable of abstract thought. This upset my teacher, and eventually I realized she just wanted me to buy into the fiction in the story of subtraction.

That is an abstract take on the business of math.

Here is another one. An old man is sitting at the water's edge and he tells his grandson that wolves are capable of great cooperation and viciousness. The little boy points out that they are wolf clan, so which are we—vicious or cooperative? The old man answered, "Whichever one you feed." This myth guides our kids to feed their cooperative side, to feed their kindness, to feed their need for communion with other beings. This is another abstraction that colonialism cannot grasp.

Mythologies from all over the world should be studied. They should be studied for the hold they have on us. Many Canadians like to pretend that as simple forest creatures we live on our mythologies. What they don't realize is that we all do. Critically studying mythology, however, might disturb our obedience to capitalism, imperialism, and patriarchy, so it is not likely to happen without a fight from inside ourselves.

Given how Canadians tend toward defensiveness rather than admitting their sins of commission and omission, that is not likely to happen.

Most Canadians think mythologies are false, are fiction, but as all writers know, fiction is often the source of profound truth. Without the fiction of zero, there would be no pyramids (which, by the way, appear in North America first), no bridges, buildings, airplanes, etc. It is also important to remember that Egyptians, the other pyramid builders, originate in southern Africa, and are Indigenous people very much like us in terms of philosophy, genius, and belief systems.

We look at mythology as the path to truth and knowledge—the key, as it were. So do Christians, but they then say theirs is the only truth and road to knowledge, which is problematic, as we all know. To dismiss mythology as of no earthly use is ludicrous. Mythology contains truth. We use fantastic stories to engage our children in the search for truth through mythology. The story of the "hole in the sky" by Ojibway people has plenty of truth. It is leading scientists to consider nuclear war here in North America. I think this is possible. The Ojibway "hole in the sky" sounds like the hole in the sky of today (the hole in the ozone layer), which may be connected to the nuclear bombing of Japan some decades ago. I am no scientist, but I am just as concerned about the viability or believability of what I am saying as I am concerned about scientists dismissing everything that is not a Western invention, belief, or myth.

Since the education of Indigenous people, scientists have begun to reconsider their cultural biases. At the Indigenous University of Quito, Ecuador, science students are coming up with new information based on old science by applying an Indigenous lens to existing science. The lens is derived from our understanding of our myths. Globally, some 45 per cent of chronic disease and 86 per cent of the burden of chronic diseases occur in people under seventy years old. This is increasing in scope and decreasing in age. There are some things science does not know about disease and death.

The serpent people teach us to think beyond ourselves, to connect wellness to the wellness around us, to connect health to being kind to one another. This is a myth, but at one time, there was a phenomenon going on in the world that birthed the myth. In the book *1491: New Revelations of the Americas before Columbus*, Charles C. Mann examines undiscussed possibilities that could have occurred to lead to various phenomena described in stories. One such phenomenon is the leaving behind of mound cities by Indigenous people. The question "Why?" could be answered by the internecine war stories from this continent.

The point is, things happened here—and they have been ignored. We have not looked at North America as a source of scientific knowledge and scientific study ever, but even the slightest examination of some beliefs and practices of Indigenous people indicate that we should. I offer a modern story. Some whales were trapped in the ice of the northern Arctic. Scientists called for the U.S. and Russia to send icebreakers. This would take weeks, maybe months, and the whales would likely perish. But the Inuit said they could sing them out. The scientists scoffed at such a ludicrous concept. They would have to admit that whales and Inuit could communicate through song. They would have to accept that the Inuit could sing whale. The scientists declined the help and continued to wait. Eventually, one of the whales died. Undaunted, the Inuit continued to go every day to tell the scientists they could sing the whales out. After the first whale died and the icebreakers were nowhere near to arriving, one scientist convinced the others to let the Inuit try.

The Inuit busied themselves cutting holes in the ice at definite intervals. When they were at the edge of the floes, they began to sing. The whales heard them and swam out to sea by following the voices. Neither the Inuit nor the scientists had a clue why this worked, but the Inuit were concerned only about getting the whales out, while the scientists wanted to study the situation. The scientists will have to wait until an Inuit child descendent from an Inuit who can sing whale songs goes to school to study science, but for that to happen, science would have to open up to the possibility that Indigenous science may have some validity.

I know that whales respond to eagle whistles. The Haida story is that a female eagle mated with a whale, and every time whales hear the eagle whistle they breach, leaping for joy in remembrance of the union. I have seen my daughter eagle-whistle several times and it always works. I am not concerned about validating this story—it has our validation. We believe it. I am concerned about studying the relationship between eagle and whale, because of other beliefs we have about these two beings.

Science has been treacherously wrong in the past. Brain size is one such fallacy. Birds—crows, to be exact—can speak two thousand languages. In the past, only Indigenous people believed animals spoke a language. We were shamed and laughed at for it. Turns out we were not wrong—science was. Some scientists are becoming concerned about their wrongness and are opening up to studying all possible sources of knowledge.

I am up with that. You do not know everything.

Conversation 5:
Hamilton

I am in Hamilton, standing in the wind. The ride here was an adventure. A transport truck spilled its cargo on the highway, and we had to find a different route to our venue, so the trip took an extra hour. I worried about being late. We had to enter Hamilton from an alternate route, and the driver did not know how to get to the GO Centre from this direction. It was a bit comic, with the driver trying to figure out aloud where to turn next and the passengers kindly offering advice and everyone beginning to fear being late. The driver let the passengers off wherever they wanted to get off, so the bus would lurch forward a little, stop, let someone off, and lurch forward again. One or two of the passengers were actually let out in the middle of the block at some store or other. In the end I was let off at a random pair of crossroads named King and John, close to the GO Centre, only I was not clear that I was near the GO Centre. My driver found me via cellphone—hurrah for math. Fiction can hothouse reality. Whether it is science fiction or literary fiction or mathematical fiction, it can alter reality and drive change. Even that was comic.

My driver was from Mozambique. I told him I remembered a Mozambican-Portuguese song I learned in the seventies and I hummed the tune. He started to sing it and I sang along. I could not believe I remembered the words to a song I did not understand; I had just liked the tune and the soft sounds of Portuguese. My sister once had a Portuguese landlord. I asked her how to say, "I am standing on my feet." She told me, and I still remember it, though I have not ever had the occasion to say it.

I am always surprised at the memory of Indigenous people. The song I was thinking of was forty-three years old in my mind. I did not say anything about the age of the song. I was glad the driver recognized it. I don't know much Portuguese, but I like the words I know. I am not sure if I sang the pair of bars I remembered correctly—it was in Portuguese, which I do not speak—but he did not challenge my brief rendition. Instead he continued to sing, looking at me all the while. The song created a bonding moment between a young Mozambican man and an elder Indigenous woman artist on a street in Hamilton beset with construction. It does not get much better than that. I am more hopeful about the change occurring between Canadians and ourselves as we reach out and meet each other.

Consequently, we had a great meeting. I love new Canadians: most of them, unless they studied North American colonization specifically, have no idea how Canada became Canada, and few know who we (as Indigenous people) are. On tour with *Bobbi Lee*, I met Amílcar Cabral, leader of the freedom movement of Guinea-Bissau. He was educated in Europe—Portugal, to be precise. He was shocked to discover there were more "Indians" in Canada than there were citizens of Guinea-Bissau. I was not very old. I could not believe how completely uninformed people were about us. One of the articles Cabral wrote that I read in the seventies before he died was about how people will resist culturally if they cannot resist either politically or physically.

Canadians do not resist culturally. They have latched onto American cultural resistance, but have rarely turned out to be cultural resisters themselves. This always surprises me. The Idle No More movement was all about cultural resistance, and it pulled a number of non Indigenous Canadians into its vortex. Hundreds of us were round-dancing in the malls of the country, taking our place anywhere we pleased in this great land, with our feet on the ground and our hands clasped in Indigenous song. Canada was shocked. No other people on this continent have been so brassy as to take their struggle to a mall—singing, dancing, and occupying it for hours. Canadians found some courage in this simple act of cultural resistance we shared the winter we danced.

There are plenty of leftists in this country but many cannot sing a single song from the great movements of the previous 150 years nor can they recite leftist poetry from their history. I can still recite the first Bliss Carman poem I ever read: "There is something in October sets the gypsy blood astir..." It still moves me, makes me want to stand up and move forward. And I can recite some of the early poetry of Indigenous poets such as Marilyn Dumont, Duke Redbird, Sky Dancer, Peter Blue Cloud, and, of course, my grandfather Chief Dan George. I love the songs we conjured from the sixties as well, and even more recently from the environmental struggles of late. I still like talking about our great artists who leapt onto the world stage with modern art, which reflected old values. We talked about this among the people who came to the gathering in Hamilton. There weren't many Indigenous people there, and a few Canadians who were curious about Indigenous people. In the end, we had a good discussion about the social responsibility of the arts. The young people reminded me of my child, Columpa Bobb—they are artists who hold up the slogan "Long Live Community and Long Live Art." I found myself with a group of diverse Canadians in a burgeoning city. I was enjoying myself. For the first time in my life I was sitting with Canadians I did not know and was having a great time.

It was also the first time I felt grateful to be born an Indigenous woman. The way forward is always clear to us. Gather together, make a plan, and create the art that will move the plan and go forward—leave no one behind.

Just the other day, some Canadian woman asked me how to increase her level of curiosity about Indigenous people. "Do something about us, with us, and for us," I replied. For instance, in Owen Sound the churches decided to ring the bells every Friday for the Murdered and Missing Indigenous Women and Girls. The town's folk got curious and invited me and John Ralston Saul to speak to them. More curiosity ensued, more ideas were born, and now the little town of Owen Sound is one of the few places in North America that rings the bells of every church on Friday at 5:00 p.m. to remind everyone of the Missing and Murdered Indigenous Women and Girls. I recall when the resistance to the MMIWG was a tiny group of women burning candles for their families on February 14 to let the world know these women were loved. I am sure such stalwart Indigenous women as writer Lenore Keeshig were a part of the movement to have the women remembered, and I was so honoured to be a part of it. The simple ringing of the bells had a big impact in the town. It had been years since I had been to Owen Sound, but the town was friendlier, more relaxed, and a comfortable place to be. It was the first time

I had been to a small town in this country and experienced the warm friendliness many non-Indigenous people speak of when they talk about small-town Canada.

I was up north giving a keynote address at the first conference on women in Nisga'a. After the keynote there was to be a feast. There are no motels or hotels in the area, so I was billeted with a woman who happened to be a Sto:lo and a relative to my children. I offered to help and she said okay. While peeling potatoes, I peeled off some of my skin. I started to bleed. "Does anyone have a Band-Aid?" I asked, and the women laughed, including myself, though I was not sure what I was laughing at, which made them laugh all the harder. "Look, she cut herself preparing her own feast. Now she is going to go down south and tell all the southerners that those ladies at Aiyansh make you prepare your honouring feast." They all laughed and so did I. I was to be honoured and there I was bleeding profusely after peeling my finger while helping to prepare for my feast. Of course, we beat the joke to death before we let it go.

I want to add a little plug for Cherie Dimaline and Sherman Alexie here. This round-robin-style humour, where everyone contributes to a joke, is common among us, but only Cherie and Sherman can do it all by themselves in their writing.

Back to the conference: someone did get me a Band-Aid. My point here is to do something. Something will happen and curiosity will be sparked up and culture will be exchanged. You find out more about the history of Indigenous feasting in Canada through preparing a feast. The women talked about the prohibition days, the early days of feast revival, and not knowing what to do because residential school had interrupted their traditional education, and all this to high notes of comedy and laughter. Joy and friendship will be sparked up. It was a powerful bonding moment for an old feminist and the women of Nisga'a.

At the gathering in Hamilton, the discussion centered on the cultural apathy of Canadians. Not surprising. In most countries, singing and dancing are common—not so much here. Someone told me that in Africa, dancing is a language. It is for us as well. When we dance, we are doing something that generations of us have been doing, and it makes us feel whole and wholly alive. We heal through song and dance. We express our deepest emotions and most powerful spirit through song and dance. We become ourselves through song and dance. We died so much during the cultural prohibition days, when our singing and dancing were banned. We are thriving now because it is legal—I am sure of that. But now we are including Canadians in the celebration of song and dance from this island, and Canadians seem more than happy to join us.

The conclusion I have come to through all of these experiences is that Canadians don't know much about us. One such Canadian asked, "How do you meet an Indian?" "I usually say hello," I replied, and the audience laughed. They know so little that they don't realize how easy it is to begin to get to know us. Not all non-Natives are in this boat. Both Dorothy Christian (Secwepemc and Syilx) and I have a friend in Victoria Freeman, author of *Distant Relations: How My Ancestors Colonized North America*. We have worked together, talked together, and are now trying to do a poetry project together, between all of our other duties. Once you have been hanging around us for a while you realize, like Victoria and Dorothy and I did, that it is complicated and difficult to truly get to know one another. But the journey is worth it. I feel that way about Canadians. You are hard to get to know and it is complicated to get to know you, but the journey is worth it.

Experiences like the above are consistent and nagging. I finally had to begin my talks with a simple truth: you don't know much about us. So few Canadians knew who we were or how we were. It took a while. It took a number of conversations with individual Canadians to get them to understand that a Sto:lo is as much like an Ojibway as a Frenchman is like a Russian.

Conversation 6:
What do I call you: First Nations, Indians, Aboriginals, Indigenous?

My first answer is "Call me anything you like, but don't call me late for dinner." Or, "Well, my name is Lee." But I know that is not what they mean. According to Columpa Bobb, "We are the only people on the continent who keep getting our names changed every ten years or so." Drew Hayden Taylor also wrote a number of funny columns about being First Nations, Indian, Aboriginal, and Indigenous, as well as Ojibway. Most of us think it is funny, this obsession with what to call us. It did not work for the world to name us, so now we are being asked who we are collectively. All of the above are designations for all of us together.

First we were called Indians because Columbus was lost, and this label hung on our necks for a long time. We had our own names for ourselves and tried to get the newcomers to use them, but to no avail—they wanted a generic name for all of us together. We objected to this name, so we became Aboriginal, as we were not in the Bible. Then some anthropologist decided we came from Asia, so we were back in the Bible, but the settlers were not done with either "Indians" or "Aboriginals," so they now had two names for us. Then someone called us Natives—that didn't last long—and then finally someone coined the term First Nations. This is the least insulting name in a long line of insulting names; it may be the most incorrect as well, but it is at least the less insulting. Of course, I am not inclined to settle for the least.

When someone asks what to call me, I want to answer: call me anything you like. I know if I answer "Sto:lo, Coast Salish" or any of our real names, someone will say, "But I mean all of you." "Well, you can do what we do," I answer. "We call you white people or Europeans because white people are from Europe. This is Turtle Island, so we are all Turtle Islanders. Why not call us 'Turtle Islanders'?"

The names derived for us are racial in nature, like Europeans, or Blacks, a generic signifier of a race of people different from the person doing the asking. There is no "all of us together," any more than Europeans are "all of you together." Turtle Island and Europe are geographical origins that name the land, not the people. We are separate nations, language groupings, and cultural groups. There are two continents of us. Having a collective term for all of us racializes us. What is the resistance of Europeans to using a geographic signature that is not of their own making? That is, we are Turtle Islanders, so why not call us that? I don't know what Indigenous people of South America call their island, but I can just bet they have a name for it.

"Indians" are from India. "Aboriginal" was coined because we are not mentioned in the Bible. We caused a great stir in the Catholic Church because we were not in the Bible. The Church could not face that the Bible could be wrong in any way, shape, or form, so it surmised that we were wrong—not original or Aboriginal. Later on, well-meaning anthropologists and priests said we are in the Bible because we are originally from Asia.

They used to teach us that we came here on a glacial ice bridge; that was one such explanation. I read it in a text as late as 1970. I asked the instructor if he had ever seen a glacier. He said no. "I have," I said. "It looks like a giant cheese wedge. So what this book is saying is that a bunch of us decided to climb this ten-mile-high glacier at one end, no pitons, no ropes, just hand over frozen hand to the top, then we slid all the way to Minnesota, eating snowfleas on the way." The Indigenous students laughed uproariously. The story was changed: there was a corridor between the two glaciers that we walked down. Now here we are, walking inside a deep freeze with ten-mile-high walls on either side—for no particular reason—all the way to southern Washington. There was no ice in the place we left, and plenty of mastodons, but we packed up to walk through a deep freeze too cold to sustain life. Now we could be as stupid as they say we are and leave a place that is not frozen to walk for miles in a place that is frozen, but I do not believe we would have survived.

Elaine Dewar, a white woman, was at a powwow watching mainly Anishinaabe people dance and decided as she watched, "I should know who these people are." After ten years of research on the origins of Indigenous people in the Americas, including researchers who had studied some of our DNA, she came to the conclusion that no one theory fits all. She published her findings in the book titled *Bones: Discovering the First Americans*. No one to this day has evidence that we came from Asia and arrived here. The Mongolians (Chinese Mongolia) believe they came from *here* and went to Asia when it was getting colder before the glacial freeze-up. This makes more sense. Science likes its bias, however, and keeps saying it is a foregone conclusion that we came from Asia. The Chinese anthropologists do not agree with the single-origin theory. Nor do the Mayan anthropologists, and of course nor do the Sto:lo. When I travelled to Mongolia, the Mongolians told us the story of them leaving North America with the horse and travelling to Siberia. We have prophecies that when the people return with the horse, this means our relatives have come back. In the Western anthropological version of the story, the dates of the arrival times vary, but the direction is always the same. We travel away from Asia, not toward Siberia. Since it was getting cold here and not in Siberia, the Mongolian story makes more sense, especially if you consider the horse disappeared here about the time it was icing over. More logical, but then science is not always about logic.

Mexicans bowed to Cortés because they thought the original people who left had returned. The Dene are linguistically tied to the Mongolians. I had the opportunity to travel to Inner Mongolia (China) with a group of Indigenous Youth. While we were in Mongolia, the Dene man we brought with us identified sixty words that were said the same and meant the same thing in both Mongolian and Dene. Further, we found out that the Dene and the Mongolians shared the same ancient songs. Simon Ortiz, poet, Diné, and guest lecturer here at the University of Toronto, told me his father could sing those songs as well. (The Dene people begin in Alaska, cross over to the North West Territories and snake their way to Mexico. There are so many different groups that there are fully nine different ways to spell Dene.) I am awed by the long-distance memory of the Dene. Fifteen thousand years and they can still sing each other's songs. Scientists would do well to give up their bias and study the secrets of memory of the Denendeh. We have no problem being related to Asians;

we do have a problem with Europeans deciding on our origins and teaching us that.

While being instructed on the glacial ice-bridge story, I asked one of my fellow northerners if his grandpa had taught him how to trap snow fleas. The Indigenous students laughed again. I wrote an essay on the topic, and it stirred some of my profs to doubt the story, but then they came up with a land-bridge idea when it was warm. Few people move without just cause. People have historically moved to "create a better life," which means they had to be having a hard time where they were. Sibir was warm when North America was freezing over. It makes no sense for people to come to North America; it makes sense for them to leave. Why would we leave Sibir?

"What should I call you?" an elder gentleman invariably asks.

"I am Sto:lo, part of the Coast Salish Confederacy," was my answer.

"No, I mean what do I call all of you?"

Answer: "Sto:lo."

"No, I mean all the Indians of this island."

"Why do you want to know?" Well, I think there is some colonial convenience in seeing us as a single entity—a mob really—and not as separate, individual nations.

"I am not sure," he answers tentatively.

We are not crazy about dealing with you separately either. It is lazy and near to useless, however, to bag all Europeans together. Ireland has about as much in common with Russia as the Crees do with the Sto:lo, but we continue to identify each other with these massive racial signifiers that make very little sense if we stop to think about it.

Lord Mercy, I am about to tell a story I don't want to tell.

One of my publishers is also my friend. I like him very much.

He was telling me about listening to Andrew Wesley at his church. Andrew is the elder of First Nations House, at University of Toronto, where I am a traditional teacher. Andrew told him a story that my mother had told me decades ago. Now, my publisher knows I grew up on story, and he knows my mother grew up in Cree country. If it was me, I would have surmised that I knew the story or I would have asked, but no such luck here. He repeated the story Andrew told him, and I didn't tell him I had heard it—at least not at first. In his email to me earlier he said, "Here I was this white settler crying away." Inside my mind I thought, "I doubt that." A gay Québécois doesn't qualify as a white settler in very many places I know about, but I didn't say that. According to poet and novelist Nicole Brossard, most Québécois are descendants of French-Algonquin mix. I continued to listen.

His conversation, my friend tells me, was about forgiveness. I have had this conversation with many Canadians. My friend and I have had this conversation before, and each time he says he gets it, but then it comes up again and I know he doesn't really get it. Forgiveness is a Christian belief, and while my friend would not insist I become a Christian, he insists on bringing up this business of forgiveness. He does not know that to accept forgiveness as a concept, I would need to convert, as forgiveness fits into the context of European belief systems. It does not fit into mine. The discussion on forgiveness is a recurring theme for him when it comes to me. He used another Indigenous man—a Christian—to launch the discussion again. I am not sure if I was clear with him, but there are many Christians who came out of residential school. There is power in being a Christian; there is no power in European society for us pagans—so this should not come as a surprise. One day I will ask him what it is he wants from me. I will be

74

so disappointed if he denies wanting anything. Denial is also very Canadian.

Along with denial goes innocence. Innocence is a recurring insistence of white people when it comes to myself and others like me—not by *me*—and so many people insist on their goodness and defend their innocence and yet they continue to live more comfortable lives, live in nicer homes, with nicer cars, more stuff, better wages, etc. This innocence comes up even over things that don't matter. Canadians fill up a room back to front, Americans fill it up front to back. One person sitting in the front pipes, "I always sit in the front—every time." I wanted to ask, "Do you want me say you are a good girl?" This denial and innocence seem to want absolution from me. But no matter what is said, Canadians of my equal do much better than me. If they are writers, they sell more books; if they are professors, they are tenured. The question of why settler Canadians get a better life off my continent than Indigenous people do does not pop into white men's heads or into the heads of other nice white women either. Do Canadians who ask about forgiveness want to be forgiven for not caring enough to be curious?

We do not have forgiveness as a recurring theme in our culture. If you hurt someone, own it, look at yourself, track where it came from, learn from it and make it right, continue to learn from it, continue to deepen your understanding, and grow from it. If you are the transgressed, look at how it made you feel, inventory how you behave, and transform yourself—do not let the transgressions of others damage your authentic self. If you were hurt, look at the impact and effect of the hurt on you and make it right inside so that later you will not pass on the hurt to those who are innocent. Continue to learn from the behaviour. How did we ever come to be a country of devastating liars who hurt and killed and continue to kill so many people without ever challenging ourselves to actually answer the first question? Worse, many people actively blame Indigenous people for their devastation. How does that work?

Who has asked what did I do or not do to make this happen? This is the question we ask when there is a conflict of any sort.

Instead, colonial white society assigned itself some crazy Knower's Chair and handed white people the authority to sit in it. They alone get to teach from this chair and decide what is true knowledge, what is false, etc. It is rare that they will give it up so that they can learn from Indigenous people or people of colour. I have a friend whom I defer to often because she knows more about her subject than I do, but she will not defer to me about my expertise and said so. I am okay with that. I am just saying that that is pretty narrow-minded. Excuse me if I have difficulty appreciating it. If I were to challenge my friend, denial would follow.

The denial maze is complicated. Part of it is about trivializing our emotional response to the insult of Canadians' refusal to give up the Knower's Chair. To assume that you as a Canadian (usually a white male Canadian) would automatically be my teacher and I your student means you have failed to see me as an emotional and mature being who might find this positioning of yourself as superior to me an insult. By making some fiction about what the insult means—*I meant no harm by it*, etc.—you eliminate my authority over my emotionality. Making up some fiction about what was intended is to deny the power and impact of what you said. To change what you said instead of owning your words is to foist the responsibility for wrongness on the person you just insulted; that is, they misunderstood you. In this way, we never get to the bottom of this thinking, this kind powering out by those who own a fictitious Knower's Chair by reason of their sex and colour over others who are the students again by reason of sex and colour. And no white men I know have ever given up the Knower's Chair willingly—they are always trying to educate me. They never seem to notice how annoying that is. I have met a few white women who have given up their Knower's Chair. That gives me some hope for the future.

You can mention any contentious subject about racism, sexism, or any other form of oppression, and your white male listener will avoid applying it to himself. Those who do that never get to experience the powerful and transformational aha moment of when you see what you are doing to up the stakes in a conflict. They will only go so far as to say yes to what you said. After that, the conversation is over. This agreement is the end of the road, and I suspect they are wanting forgiveness. There will be no discussion of the origin of the admission, no discussion of its history and effect on the individual. The thing that moves them is forgiveness. For what? To be forgiven, the transgressor has to confess, but that did not happen, so does this mean the tearful white man is shedding tears of relief? After all, his place is intact, the Knower's Chair is still his, and he does not have to change anything. But if I admit to something, he sometimes uses it against me in the future to defend himself.

We live in such a convoluted, invasive, and dispirited culture. And so few are responsible for its creation or transformation. I was given the position of keynote speaker at an education conference at York University. The audience was majority (women) people of colour. Before me there was a panel. Every single person on the panel was white. They were all female. I almost chuckled. Forty years ago, that would have been a line of white men. Actually, only fifteen years ago a line of white men were called upon to talk about Indigenous women. In any case, I realized white people had not given up the Knower's Chair, they just changed the gender of its occupant. I thought, you invited the wrong person for the keynote, and talked for an hour about the Knower's Chair. I am not the sort of badger you bring into the rabbit hole. Colonialism had consigned the business of knowing to itself. So white people can say things that are unverified. I decided to make the keynote a speech about the Knower's Chair and how we need to kick it off the stage. This is why we say white man don't listen.

I would be dispirited but for those Canadians struggling with "ally-ship." Most Canadians think it is enough to know something, but this is not enough—you must commit to the continued growth and transformation of whatever you claim to know.

Not long ago we were discussing how to word future hires. "What is it we really need?" one of the committee members asked. "Cultural competence," I answered. "It is not enough to acknowledge the culture—you must commit to its continued growth and transformation." *Aha*—again, another aha moment, this time in a multicultural group that included a white woman who gave up her Knower's Chair—then the discussion changed from tense parrying to joint development.

Conversation 7:
Galloping toward Ottawa

This book was written on my iPhone. I was travelling so much during its writing that I decided to use the Notes section on my phone to draft each paragraph. It feels like we are on horseback galloping toward Ottawa. We can't land in Toronto due to severe thunderstorms, and I am thinking about my friend Dawnis Kennedy.

Dawnis is an Ojibway Midewiwin healer and a lawyer who studied western law and Anishinaabe law. Actual Indigenous law, not the treaties and various bits of Canadian legislation that gets called Indian law, but actual Anishinaabe oratorical law. Kennedy audited my class while studying for her PhD in law at the University of Toronto. We found ourselves locked in our worlds of law from time to time—alternately serious and hilarious as we laid out our thinking. Dawnis would jump up and join me teaching, writing on my blackboard, standing on my Knower's Chair, and not one person in that class thought this was odd. In fact, when I wasn't able to make it to class one day, the class soldiered on without me. The Knower's Chair had become a mere shadow of itself—it had no power over these students. That is what I seek in every class I teach.

Hilarity surfaced in moments when we stumbled on those things we would never agree on—like Ojibway women wearing the long skirts of the previous century during ceremony. Anishinaabe women dress in the nineteenth-century style of Ojibway/European dress—a long skirt without either the sexy bustle of European women or the leathers of traditional Indigenous women.

West coast women like to dress up—the cultural art forms are still there but the style is Euro-modern-chic. We both laughed as Dawnis said that my people would ask her, "Are you going to put on your Amish getup and come to ceremony with us?" by way of inviting her to longhouse. We cracked up along with the whole class. I have no idea what we all found so funny—Ojibway Amish ways or the pretentiousness of the Sto:lo. No matter: we so enjoyed our difference. During the years of working with the left on the west coast, my experience was the opposite. White people wanted everyone to think like them and would spend hours arguing over every little word in every leaflet they made. It grew so tiring, and eventually the group would break up.

I bring Dawnis up as both a Canadian and an Anishinaabe. We presented together at the University of Toronto, and she articulated in the clearest and most reasonable way that she had two heritages: a Canadian one and an Ojibway one, and she was entitled to both. I remember thinking along those lines many years ago. But I did not respect being a Canadian for reasons I explain in another chapter. But do Canadians have this duality as well?

Normally, when you migrate to another country, you pick up the host language, pick up your new culture's customs. Most people don't give up their cultures and customs, but try to integrate into the world they have moved to. No such thing in North America. The idea of "going Indian" is laughable, seen as a caricature—"playing Indian"—because we are perceived to be docile forest creatures, not real nations with citizenship requirements and a naturalization process. We did have such a process; it was handled by elders, particularly women, who culturally assimilated newcomers into our world. But the assumption by England that we were not real countries made it ludicrous to Europeans to integrate into our nations, so it did not happen. Even today, a person who is white and integrates into Indigenous society is perceived to be a fraud, even if the nation accepts them. Even some of us who claim to be nations will bloodline anyone they think is faking it. You can no longer become one of our citizens, Canada said so, and now we are buying it. We do so at our peril. Canada does not allow it, because if it did, that would make us nations. So those who stick to the bloodlines are siding with the colonizer against our nationhood.

Canadians think they are nice, but they absolutely hate sharing the country with us. When they ask us to forget the past and integrate, they are really expressing their hate for sharing the land base. When I examine the original meaning of *nice*, it makes me wonder why Canadians want to be considered that. When they came here, northern Turtle Island would not be called Canada for 250 years. The names were ours, the language spoken between us was Indigenous and Chinook, and the settlers also spoke their own languages among themselves. The pressure to anglicize came after the French-English war. We were forced to anglicize; even Quebec is fairly Anglo. Still, that does not change the fact that we are entitled to both of our heritages. I always say that everyone here belongs here, but non-Indigenous people have only one heritage: a Canadian one. They do, however, have a secondary responsibility: an Indigenous responsibility. The problem with assigning them this responsibility is that we would have to consider ourselves nations with the power to assign citizenship or to naturalize citizens and confer upon them national citizenship in the same ways Canada, England, Egypt, or any other country does to its new citizens. We don't.

What do we hate—white people who love our language and culture?

This is changing as our languages are taught at universities in Canada. But we rely on Canada for our definition of who is an Indigenous person or national citizen. Let's face it: the "status" Indians have the edge. Canada decided that Canada alone had the right to determine nationhood, citizenship, membership, and status. Because status Indians had the edge, the rest of us had to fall in line or be quiet. I refused to be quiet, but I was sixty before my father and siblings "recognized" me. I paid no attention to my relations who relied on the state for who we are. I was not a victim of residential school so did not suffer the shame or cultural denial of those who were. I knew a great deal more about our culture than others did, but I did not have the right to brag about that, so I wrote stories.

Fiction.

Fiction is powerful truth.

Conversation 8:
Jack Scott and the left

Here we are, 150 years of Canadian colonialism, and Indigenous people have been reduced to a race-based identity through Hitler-style politics coming from the outside and sometimes from the inside. You can't be an "Indian" unless the colonial government, the settler population, and their identity police say you are.

No, I am not a Canadian. I could not continue to elect government after government that did nothing to stop the earth-pillaging that is going on now. So much research has shown that we are on the brink of a mass extinction event, and still Canada seeks to develop oil, gas, and uranium reserves. Every time someone asks me if I consider myself a Canadian, I want to say, "Seriously? You came from another country, asked for a place to say, then you soon removed whatever people were left over from the diseases you shared with us." In the very first settlement on the east, the British collected twenty-four dollars in excise tax and trade from Indigenous people; they spent one dollar on the Indigenous people, twenty-one dollars on the colony, and took the rest home for the king. The Indigenous people were by far the majority, but it mattered little: it was a matter of who deserved what. This ratio has not changed, except for the worst. There is a mine in Innu country; it produces $1.5 billion in wealth every year. The Innu get exactly zero from that mine; a significant amount is washed out among Canadians.

The eastern Arctic Dene, who have been negotiating for a permanent reserve since the 1950s, have been chased all over the Arctic for seventy-five years now. Every time they move to an area where the caribou pass through, the federal government moves them again. Some environmentalist do-gooder told the feds that it is the Indigenous people who are endangering the eastern Arctic caribou. Hence the Dene must move instead of eating. When they formed their own government, the Inuit gave the Dene 10,000 acres so they could pursue their hunting-and-gathering lifestyle. But this does not stop Canada from moving them when the caribou come by.

The Dene also suffer from so much disease—TB, influenza, and pneumonia—and we have been through successive governments—Liberal and Conservative—but nothing has changed for the Dene. In the northern parts of Ontario and Manitoba, where there is so much water, Indigenous people are in the midst of a water crisis—still think I should want to be a Canadian? When the Indigenous people complained about the inability of the feds to maintain their water promise, Harper sent them buckets, so in minus-zero winter weather for seven months of the year, the Indigenous people haul water, some of them for more than ten miles.

"What?" says the Canadian. "Why don't they move?"

I get that. That was your solution to oppression everywhere in the world—move, run away, I am outta here. It is not ours.

We are responsible for the land we have been on for thousands of years; we cannot relinquish our responsibility. We are the land's caretakers. This has been our continent for thousands of years. Some of our people wish Canadians would move back to their original homelands. Not me—I hope they fall in love with the land the way I have: fully, responsibly, and committed for life.

Even if we could afford it, the Canadian state does not entitle us to dig holes in the ground and create running water ourselves. Every bit of something we do must be accompanied by a Band Council Resolution signed by the minister of Indian affairs, whom Canadians elect. We do not get to elect our own government. You elect our government. We elect a band council that is beholden to your government, the Canadian government.

We are handed programs that change year to year, so if you worked in one program this year, it may disappear next year, in which case you will be on Employment Insurance. This is the deliberate destabilization of our economic opportunities, something that does not happen anywhere else. All other Canadian towns and cities have budgets, the same line items every year, except in those years when the town gets something special like transit. So if you get a job working the roads as a labourer, you may continue until you retire—this allows you to financially plan. No such opportunity exists for us. The only people who benefit from our budgets are consultants, who are invariably white.

The diamond mine in Attawapiskat brings in $6 billion a year, of which the federal government receives a significant share, but it pays only $1 million to Attawapiskat. The lowest jobs at the mine go to the Crees, who receive a wage not anywhere near commensurate with that of the Canadians who also work for the diamond mine. These corporations are in Innu and Cree territories. Some thirty years ago or so, the federal government declared that the subsoil rights did not belong to Indigenous people, so the government did not have to share royalties with the nations on whose land they mined. Many Indigenous people began blocking roads to the mines and suffered much for that.

I have met a number of leftists, and they are not loyal to their government, but they are loyal to the notion of Canada—the current colonizer, their country. I made friends with some of them. I shared a house with two of them. I am still friends with one of the two people I shared a house with many decades ago. I was friends with Jack Scott until he passed into the spirit world.

The leftists I met seemed to be allies in a common struggle to change Canada into something radically different. The Indigenous people asked the two white guys about the left and they did not know the history of the left in Canada. But they wanted to, and they knew someone who could teach us.

They explained who Jack Scott was—a prominent theoretician on the left who was a follower of Mao Zedong. We liked that idea. I mean, if you are going to like some communists, let's like some communists of colour was my immature thinking at the time. My husband was aware of the differences between one leftist group and another. He was a young Trotskyist at one point, then a Mao supporter, but he was never anti-Trotsky even as a Mao supporter, so he hoped to engage in reasonable conversation with a fellow Mao supporter and he thought Jack Scott might fit that bill.

I and my partner were also curious about why some leftists were so anti-Trotsky. I didn't know who any of these people were, so I started reading my husband's books. My roommates did not agree on the value of reading. One of them overrated it and the other underrated it, so talking about what I was reading with them was out of the question. My husband did not really agree that women should be reading anything—he was a sexist at the time—so talking to him was out. I read when he was at work. I was pregnant so not working. Lucky me.

Before my first child was born, my partner and I, and a cousin of mine named Henry Jack, were living as a collective with Steve Whalen and Mike Russell on 37th and Culloden near Knight Street in Vancouver. They were young leftists. None of us actually trusted them; no white man we knew would stand with us in the face of opposition to other white folks. Steve was cut from a different cloth though. He ended up going to Wounded Knee. He found it amusing no one had asked him if he was white—all the Indigenous people assumed he was Indigenous, and he didn't tell them any different. He also found this amusing. He and Mike argued over us a lot, and so finally Mike moved out—we never saw him again. In between us moving in, my daughter being born, and Mike moving out, we all decided to ask the Progressive Workers Movement to give us an oral history of the left and the union movement.

Jack Scott came to give us that history. When he finished his tea, he put the cup on its saucer very gently and began: "First, you need to know that BC unions were built on white supremacist principles for the most part. Marx had not anticipated that." From his brogue, it was clear Jack was Gaelic. "Second, Canada was farm country—two-thirds agrarian until the Second World War. Pretty much semi-illiterate when the labour movement began. This was a summation of the condition of the working class in Canada in general and in BC in particular."

It was somewhat magical to have a whole bunch of white folks in our living room being educated by Jack Scott. He talked about the near revolution in Russia and its effect on the left, the communist party's "Take an Indian to lunch" program as a recruitment tool and as an attempt to fight racism from within the working class. He talked about Nadezhda Krupskaya, Lenin's wife, educating the working class of Russia. He read her book on the pedagogy of the working class and used the lessons in it to educate Canadian workers during the Depression. Most of the workers were farm boys joining the working class as unemployed—not really workers like the people in Krupskaya's book, but he found the book useful nonetheless. The big thing he said was he had to get over himself. He laughed copiously and we laughed carefully, so as not to be disrespectful. He had a powerful memory, an ordered mind, and was a clear orator.

Jack brought other leftists over a six-week period and they taught us the history of the working class of Canada. We heard about the betrayals by union leaders of their workers and betrayals by Communist Party leaders of their members. We learned about other smaller leftist groups and movements that came and failed. I noticed that always the weakness came from within. I surmised this weakness was connected to the damage and hurt the oppressed group that had not healed felt as a result of their oppression.

Trauma affects belief. The workshops made this plain, though Jack would not agree with me. I have, however, lived my life with this story and it has served me well. The seeds of defeat come from within the damage bestowed on the whole.

What preceded these workshops was the sixties. A lot has been said about that decade of Buffy Sainte-Marie and Bob Dylan. There are others tied to those two, but those are the two who really affected the world and left a very large footprint in their breath tracks. The sixties was a heady time for a lot of people, none more so than Indigenous people. Some people viewed us as human, not to be beaten but to be discovered. While we were not keen on being discovered all over again, it was better than the 1950s. We began thinking too. We came together in small groups full of thoughts and questions and struggled for answers.

I remembered walking down the street in 1969 thinking I was a character from *The Wizard of Oz* who had been given a brain. I was ecstatic. I wasn't the only one; instead of just one old scarecrow getting a brain, hundreds and thousands of us had got one. That is the Indian way. It was as if someone opened our minds and all kinds of thoughts came tumbling out about colonialism, racism, sexism, and homophobia—although that last phenomenon remained a bit of an anomaly until this decade.

What surprised me about Jack Scott was his affection for Stalin. I thought of old Tim Moody, member of the Squamish Nation and friend to my family, who said he had no problem with killing people who were trying to wreck the country, but his problem with Stalin was that Stalin decided this on his own. Like a king, not like a person. We used to have slaves, he explained, but then mass death occurred—probably an epidemic from the East—and we decided to give up slavery. It made us give up a lot of other things too—like kings, queens, nobility, upper clans, etc. But the most important one for Tim was that we gave up making all the decisions as heads of our families and began a long process of consultation among us. We are still learning about democracy from that one decision.

The Indigenous people listening to the workshops had a few problems with Stalin, and this led us to read Marx and Lenin more deeply and not take someone else's word. We needed to read this with ourselves in mind. "So who are we?" became the question we constantly asked. To paraphrase Marx, from out of the old comes the new. This struck me and made me ask questions: what are our laws, our politics, our ethics, and our principles? Answering those questions took a different kind of reading. Instead of copying someone else's politics, we researched social movements and learned about the nature of social change, including our own. We are ex-slavers. I had to talk to my elders again—I will never forget that. That wasn't who my husband was; his people never did have slaves, and that led me to realize we are different nations, or we are one nation with many cultures, or we are many nationalities with a single vision. We needed to settle something here before we could go on. And that was exciting to all of us.

The Canadians we then talked to begin to change. We didn't talk to just any random Canadian; we talked to the left, different branches of the left. Each of us had his or her favourite theoretician, thinker, and revolutionary. It was rather fun. Each of us would read different thinkers on the same subject, then we would get together and talk about it. I like that we were in no hurry to settle on anything. In the meantime, we started to look at our own people more or less critically. The left's questions changed: no more "What are you going to do, drive us into the sea?" Instead, we were asked questions about nationhood, liberation, independence, secession and whether or not we were minorities, tribes, internal colonies and so forth.

Most of the leftists I met back then are no longer leftists. Jack Scott stayed true to himself till the end. I stayed true to him too, not that I adopted his politics per se, but I was his friend till his end.

I never stopped wondering why Jack liked Stalin so much, but I never asked him. He was especially happy when he said, "Stalin would have solved things in Stalin's way: shorten him by a head." It made me slightly afraid of him. Is this the end run of advocating violent revolution, rather than sticking with social transformation? Am I a peacenik? A Ghandiist? I don't think so. I am a Sto:lo. I have no problem with physical fighting, but it is not something I advocate. We are ready for all eventualities. The saying is: *We are ready. We are always ready. We fear nothing.* We believe if we die too soon, we will be back with another chance at life. I believe this, deeply. So violence is not something I build into my plans. I am the daughter of the princess of peace. Peace is the foundation of our organizing efforts. Unlike Martin Luther King Jr., I would not stand idly by while white men in hoods bombed small girls in a church, but I also would not arm myself like the Panthers did. Everything is about perception and perception that counts comes from someone else. I am sure Martin Luther King Jr. got busy when those little girls were bombed, but I only saw an inactive response. I did not criticize King any more than I would challenge Jack. First, this was my perception and it could be flawed, and for Jack I said little because I did not want our friendship to end. He was round about my stepfather's age and mostly a courageous and gentle soul, unlike my stepdad, and I did not want that interrupted. Asking him might have made him mad. That was the only time I did not risk someone's wrath over a question, a statement, or a thought.

I do recall on one occasion telling Jack that Canadians would not know who they were unless they studied how they got here. He nodded assent to that. He included what he knew about the diasporic migrations of non-Native people to North

America and the difference between Canadian settlement and US settlement. This put me closer to the discussion, as it was something I was passionately interested in and studying kind of chronically.

Conversation 9:
Divisions, constraints and bindings

Homophobia and Gender

The first division of patriarchy is between men as gender and women as gender and the gender-fluid, and then the first constraint of patriarchy is on homosexuals and the gender-fluid, then on women. The first binding is the gender woman to the gender man—all humans are forced to identify as either man or woman. This declaration is a binding agent, and they must bind. No other binding is legitimate. The madness is that the divided are bound without negotiation, fairness, or agreement and spend most of their life quarrelling about the binding union. One half of the divided are constrained along with those who do not fit the gender binary. Every five or ten years half the population divorces one another and the binding begins again, again without much in the way of negotiation about the power relations, the dynamic, or the rules of engagement. Men and women who are homophobic absolutely hate that homosexuals may not be unfairly or inequitably bound together. The suspicion that they have something we cannot, as heterosexuals, have is not lost on me.

Most heterosexuals see the oppression of homosexuals as unfair and unjust but do not see themselves as gendered individuals who are bound by their gender; this binding is part of the conundrum and driving force of homophobia that they are connected to. The problem to Indigenous people is gendering everything, and that is connected to patriarchy or the initial division. Forcing us to gender ourselves is the first unfair binding and constraint.

I am awed on some level by my former partner, who saw herself as a woman trapped in a man's body. She felt like a woman. That must be so transformative, so liberating—I have no idea how a gender feels. I am often asked about matriarchal power and how roles work in our nation. There is power. We agree on that. When that Sto:lo (Fraser River) comes crashing through Hell's Gate canyon at two million gallons per minute, that is power. "Take your place" is power. I choose to mother children. I take my place in their mothering. No man or woman would try to usurp it unless I did not take it. If I fail to take my place as a mother, my children will be neglected, and no one in my village or family will allow that to happen: someone will step up. If you want to be powerful, then you take your place, execute your responsibilities in a powerful way. This is not gendered.

Although I am not gendered into a role and do not know how it feels to be gendered, I do know how it feels to be a sexual being, to be aroused, to want to be with another human being. I do know I love penile penetration, the feel of the penis on my body, and I am not so crazy about non-penile-penetration forms of sex. I also know that heterosexuals engage in homosexual-style sexual acts. None of this confuses me. I do understand that some people were born as male and feel female. They have that extraordinary gift of feeling gendered.

That is so powerful to me, I respect that. I am, in fact, awed by it. It is a gift to the nation. This has nothing to do with "roles." Roles are stilted. Static, they are bound, held together by rules. This is not us. Fluidity is the absence of rules and roles. No boxes to stuff your being in. There is recognition that we are not the same, but we have common beliefs and common goals—the wellness of the nation.

I become confused when I am asked to identify my gender. Although my sexual proclivities, attractions, enjoyments, etc., are clear to me, the feeling of being a gendered individual is not. I am aroused by the deep, low tones of Salish men when they sing. I am also attracted to the high notes men hit when they sing in Cree or Anishinaabe—it excites me. The accepted gendered male body attracts me, arouses me, but I have had heterosexual men look at me with shock when I ask them how it feels to be a gendered man. If my former partner was transgendered, then I am female-gendered. I need a language that speaks fairly and justly and somewhat neutrally to all of this, and English is not it.

This is another case for having everyone learn an Indigenous language. No pronouns. No gender divisions, no gender bindings, and no constraints. And yet I cannot imagine how this would work in English.

Beyond female gendering:
Who do we leave out when we gender-role women?

In 2015, I was asked to contribute to a chapter of a book. *Beyond Women's Words* I think was the title. I am borrowing it and altering the title for this book instead. *Beyond Women's Words* is such a strong and an extraordinary title, and I have a feeling it means something quite different to me than perhaps to others who are going to read this book. In so much of the language of race, space, and justice in Canada, as it applies to Indigenous women, our gender(s) are silent or absent or unspoken of, so when I consider what is Beyond Women's Words after having been left out for so long, or ignored, or treated as a footnote to justice, I feel like I have just been discovered. It is only recently that we have been referred to in the press as Indigenous women and not female native, like a female dog or some other such animal. I also feel like I am beginning to discover other genders. When did women realize we have a gender called "woman" among us? I would think it would be the moment we discovered transgendered women and transgendered men. It is the transgendered who help us to see ourselves.

When was it for Europeans? Was it following patriarchy and the privileging of the male gender, the underprivileging of women and transgendered individuals? More important, when did people decide women were germane to their text? Did women who include us in *Beyond Women's Words* realize we read these articles with a degree of melancholy? Do gender-fluid beings and transgendered beings read this section with a certain amount of melancholy? "There is no future in yesterday, so let us advance" (Mahmoud Darwish). I am compelled to respond to the words in my own text.

We have moved from silence to voice to activism around women in the past three decades. Women have built organizations or created art around the principle of Indigenous female equality. We are conscious as artists that Canada still murders Indigenous women four times as often as any other race of women in this country. Our work is driven by both experience and words, but we have moved beyond words, to do the sorts of things that will enrich the lives of Indigenous women. We are aware that it has taken us decades to get an inquiry into why our murders are the least investigated and why we are the least protected. Part of the work of this inquiry will include the investigation of police accused of violating Indigenous women instead of protecting them. And part of the work will sit with connecting racism, sexism, patriarchy, homophobia, and feminism to the murders.

As I answer the questions Canadians have put before me, my own questions are being born. What happens when sharing and caring meet exploitation and invasion? Now I am beginning to wonder: why did it take twenty-six years to have our calls for an inquiry responded to? I do hope some Canadian takes on this responsibility in answering my question.

Conversation 10:
Appropriation

Most people seem to be using appropriation when they include a Native character in their story. One of the people who was accused of appropriation in the 1980s was the author of *Dance Me Outside*, W. P. Kinsella. I was asked about his work often after arguing against appropriation at the 1988 International Feminist Book Fair in Montreal. Two things happened at the fair. One was that I asked the feminist movement as a whole to move over. I did not ask Anne Cameron, who wrote *Daughters of Copper Women*, to move over. I asked Anne Cameron to stop stealing our stories. We talked together for several hours. Like other people (white people), she thought if some elders asked her to write our stories down that it was okay with the rest of us.

What our elders did not know, and I know no white person has ever explained to them, is that once you give away the story, that is it, your children are disinherited. Some elders don't mind that but some do, and that should have alerted the white writer to something being wrong here. Who would give away their children's inheritance if they were aware that

that is what they were doing? It would have to be someone who is alienated from the children. A caring person would ask, how is it that some of our elders do not know they are giving up their children's inheritance? Instead people—particularly white people who are offered the heritage of Indigenous children—salivate with pride and go ahead and plunder it. Shame on you.

I was at my ex-husband's home not long ago and he seethed with rage as he asked, "What is it with your people fighting over names?" and he spat out a common North American curse. I answered, "We did not own property and we gave away all our possessions during potlatch and potlatched as often as possible in our lifetime. All we owned was our stories, our songs and our names—this is our private, clan, family wealth. That was our private property. In the songs of Y-Ail Mihth translated by Eloise Street and orated by Goldensnake Sepass, the history of the Sto:lo is recounted, as told by us, remembered by us, and lived by us. It declares who we are and what we believe, where we have been and where we are now. It is our bible. For some white person to come along and say, 'Chief so-and-so gave it to me,' is to disinherit us of who we are. We can no longer say, 'I am the granddaughter of the singers of the songs of Y-Ail Mihth. I am without property, inheritance, or citizenship.' The possession of the songs, the stories, and the names is as sacred as the Bible, your home, and your passport—altogether.

Everyone in the world would laugh if I said, "I just wrote this great book, I think it is a bestseller. It starts out: *Verily, verily I say unto you.*" Everyone would say, "That is already written," and laugh at me. But if someone writes *Daughters of Copper Women* and signs her name to it and collects the royal coinage for it (copyright and royalties), no one laughs. It is an Indian story and she is entitled to steal that, just like Indian property, Indian names, etc. Everything we own is up for grabs. In 1988, we said, "No more theft."

The intention of appropriation is stealing, so in order for appropriation to occur, theft must travel with it and receive either resale for profit or personal royalties as benefit from its use. Theft must be the outcome for the appropriator, while the original owner must lose the use, benefit, authority, and ownership (as control) over the appropriated item; otherwise it is simply sharing. We are teaching our languages to everyone—that is not appropriation. English was forced on us—that is not appropriation. It is offered by the owners of the language and we pay to learn it—it cost us a continent. Appropriation can occur only if the person doing the appropriating has no prior authority or birthright or permission to access the item and no permission from its original owner to use or benefit from the item.

During the colonization of Canada, both land and knowledge were appropriated—that is, expropriated without permission from the owners. On the one hand, we were separated from our knowledge, and on the other, Europeans were entitled to appropriate the knowledge associated with the use of items they purchased. For instance, Johnny Whiteman purchases squaw vine for his wife's menopausal condition from Lee's gramma. He copyrights the knowledge he acquires. Lee is sent to school and cannot access her gramma's knowledge about squaw vine while away because she is separated from her gramma and someone else owns the copyright of the information. Gramma dies while Lee is in school. Johnny Whiteman publishes a book and includes the squaw vine knowledge of Lee's gramma, and on her return from school Lee learns that in order for her to access her gramma's knowledge, she must purchase Johnny

Whiteman's book. She is purchasing from the appropriator access to her inheritance.

Johnny Whiteman receives all royalties from the sale of the book, while Lee, the intended inheritor of the intellectual property of her gramma, must now contribute to the wealth Johnny Whiteman gained by having access to her gramma while she was separated from her. Now Lee was in residential school, which neither her mother, her father, or grandmother agreed to, as they were children in the eyes of the law. The grandmother did not think she was disinheriting her granddaughter. The white people who took the knowledge told her gramma that Lee could use it if she wanted to. And that was true, as long as she was willing to pay for it. The universities of this country own most of our knowledge, and Indigenous people must buy it back as courses.

Universities are using the book in their coursework. Researchers at the university examine the humble squaw vine and find the "active ingredient" in it, name it in Latin, and claim to have "invented" it. Now more white men are benefiting from Lee's gramma's knowledge while Lee is separated from the possibility of isolating the active ingredient herself, because as yet she is not entitled to secure the research grant and engage in the process of isolation in the same way white men are.

Now Johnny Whiteman, a group of researchers, the institution, and the public have benefited financially from the theft of Lee's birthright while Lee has been left out in the cold with no inheritance. Now any white man can figure this out, it is their system of plunder. Not so our people. We operate on truth and belief; if you tell my grandmother I can use something once she gives it to you, she believes you. If you don't tell her that I will have to pay for it, because you own it, you have appropriated our cultural knowledge and separated my grandmother's grandchildren from inheriting it. This was never the intention of our grandmothers. White people in the process of acquiring our cultural knowledge never told our ancestors the consequences of the decision they were making. In this way it is unconscionable and it is still stealing. In fact, stealing is embedded in the definition of appropriation.

We currently must purchase our original medicines (herbal and many herbal medicine–based pharmaceuticals are Indigenous) and our medical knowledge from non-Indigenous people who do not recognize our authorship of this knowledge. For this appropriation to have been possible, the authority of the original people had to be abrogated and usurped by the official representatives (the Crown) of the would-be appropriators and Indigenous access to the knowledge and land severed; as well, the appropriated authority had to be rationalized and maintained. That is the very nature of how colonialism works.

The rationale for this complicated fraud was threefold: first, non-recognition of the validity of Indigenous governance; second, the infantalization of the oral nature of Indigenous knowledge as not deserving of the same recognition and protection as written knowledge; and third, the dismissal of the Indigenous relationship to the land as non-ownership and non-civilized—that is, non-private property. Private property is the foundation of citizenship and civilization in European society, and intellectual property is an extension of private property. While the power of our names, our stories, and our songs is what our inheritance is about.

Following the successful appropriation of Indigenous authority and the separation of Indigenous children from their parents, grandparents, etc., and from their knowledge, deliberately, through epidemic death, residential schools, and the new governing body (chief electoral system) established by the Indian Act and enforced by the Department of Indian Affairs, we lost access to land, knowledge, proprietorship, and the benefits that accrue to continued inherited access to land, and knowledge's development.

At the time of pre-emption, when white men were offered Indigenous people's land, Indigenous people were not entitled to purchase land or pre-empt land and were restricted to reservations with one-fifth the amount of land per family compared to that allotted to white people. People of colour, such as Blacks and Asians, were entitled to purchase much less per family but they could purchase land—this means everyone got ahead of us. Indigenous people were further prohibited from transmitting and practicing culture (which included transmitting knowledge and singing and dancing, telling stories, hosting meetings, gatherings, getting married, etc.). At the same time, Indigenous people were not permitted to attend Western institutions of higher learning, such as public school or university, or accrue wealth and land in a European manner, i.e., through purchase. We were declared uncivilized and uncivilizable; our land and our knowledge were deemed (white) public domain to be exploited by Johnny Whiteman and his cohorts and descendants. This gave a decided advantage to certain white men. A single white man purchased our mountains, from North Vancouver to Pemberton, BC, for twenty-five dollars—Whistler, Grouse Mountain, the Lions, and Mount Seymour were among them, all of which are multimillion-dollar profit-bearing ski resorts now.

Children were separated from knowledge keepers. The use of land and open (rivers, lakes and oceans) water for sustenance was controlled by the Indian agent, who often prohibited the use of rivers, lakes, and oceans by the Indigenous adult population for food gathering. Following the separation of children from adults, and adults from the land, a hostage-based treaty-making process was set into motion (which was successful everywhere but in BC until recently), and Indigenous people were declared "as infants" in the eyes of the law, infantilized and managed by white men. This infantalization and the concomitant Indian agent and residential school system were used to maintain the Crown's authority and the separation of children from the adult population. Upon returning, the children were adults and began families; work separated them from elders, and they in turn were separated from their children, until alienation and internal violence overtook the original caring and sharing between Indigenous people and their families.

At the same time, only Europeans were entitled to attend university, which is where our knowledge was concentrated, and only they could access it. They then could write about us, so they became our experts and we began to believe we were inferior. Inevitably and predictably, the children returned from residential school languageless, and over time, because the knowledge was not transmitted to children, we began to think we did not have much knowledge. I can remember Indigenous people telling me we had no science, to which I responded, "So what is space-logging then—home economics?"

Our children are no longer able to speak the language that connected them to the land, articulated their authority over its care, and identified and defined the knowledge attached to its use. The base (of knowledge) atrophied, grew smaller. Further, the pass system prohibited interaction between communities, such that the exchange of knowledge, the discourse between knowledge keepers and common knowledge, its growth and development were arrested.

In the meantime, different types of alter-Native medicine have developed since Johnny Whiteman first appropriated Lee's gramma's knowledge and the nature of discussion between us has atrophied. We still wonder whether or not we had si-yams, clan heads, and traditional chiefs, or did we just have elders? We wonder whether or not we had science. We wonder whether or not we should give tobacco to our elders when we go and speak to them, or should we bring food? When I was little, my Ta'ah did ask me for tobacco. I brought my mother's bannock; Ta'ah held it, shook it a little, smiled, and said, "Best." This is one of her few English words. Then she put it in her cupboard. It was my gift to her and she knew it. It was payment for whatever knowledge she chose to transmit. She knew that too and so did I. Sometimes I came with bannock and a can of fish. She twirled when I gave it to her and put it in her cupboard. I was paying for the knowledge. This is part of our tradition.

Today we struggle to reclaim our knowledge, to articulate and create literary and scholarly works from it, and to end the theft through writing that characterized 120 years of prohibition, theft, and abrogation of our ancestors' authority and ownership of knowledge. For us to reclaim knowledge, we must have access to it, we must re-aggregate it and we must build institutions to accomplish this. Protection before aggregation of our intellectual property will only lead to an atrophied or crippled and limited rebirthing of our original knowledge base. No one grandmother knows what all the grandmothers once knew. Our knowledge was collectively held. Our fire has been hit, the logs scattered. With the scattering of our logs, so is our knowledge scattered. We need to assemble ourselves as our ancestors once did (powwow) and hold a series of discussions (conferences) exchanging what we know and rebuilding the knowledge base. We must ensure that our children and grandchildren have access to this process of Indigenous knowledge acquisition from beginning to end.

At the same time, we must protect our knowledge from those who wish to continue the theft without our permission. We must be cognizant of the need for protection, while still wary of getting so caught up in the business of protection that we create the sorts of protocols, rules, and regulations that inhibit our willingness and ability to transmit knowledge to our descendants. Protocols are for foreigners, particularly those who have a history of appropriation; they are not for our children. On the other hand, I am unwilling to volunteer ourselves up for any further theft. Protection from abrogation and appropriation while assuring transmission is tricky.

We need to know who we are, who we once were, and who we will always want to be (as my uncle Lenard George always says). First, we need to address our relationship to the land and to one another not as nuclear families, but as extended longhouse families. Second, we interacted not merely from within longhouse families, but the extended longhouse families had relationships to other extended longhouse families who lived inside villages, and they interacted with each other. Each village had relations with other villages from other nations who interacted village to village. A complex recognition system developed between the various si-yams that existed between each village and within the nation. This system included the covenants between us and the processes and extent of sharing, exchanging, and transmitting knowledge, thinking, stories, songs, and so forth. They were recited at gatherings by rememberers. Over time, certain villages became known for certain types of expertise (horticultural, aquacultural, medical, etc.), and the sharing and exchange of valued items, knowledge, and services led to the formation of a confederated interactive group of *Friendly* people who spoke the same language—not literally, of course, but they shared terms and a common philosophical perspective, a common understanding and a shared foundation of fairness, equal exchange in trade, recognition, or ownership, territoriality and mutual benefit. We then formed confederated groups that could communicate in a way that was based on shared understanding, shared story, and shared naming. We could make deals, agree on terms, and interact easily.

Our pragmatic sensibility led to the creation of confederated organs of recognized and shared authority, which carried out duties and responsibilities in accordance with recognized expertise and familiarly owned knowledge, stories, songs, and intellectual property. The customs and conditions for sharing the foregoing and exchanging the foregoing were agreed upon in varying degrees by all of those people living inside the territory shared by Coast Salish people. Those who agreed less, interacted less—there was never a sentiment of discord over lack of agreement. This enabled the social, cultural, creative, intellectual, medical, scientific, and economic interaction between the *Friendly* nations of the west coast, now known in English as Coast Salish people. (Some people prefer the original languages. I am told by Kevin Paul, author of *Little Hunger*, which was short listed for the Governor General's Literary Award for Poetry in 2009, that his people prefer the original language to describe themselves. I respect that.)

Jurisdiction over land, production, caretaking, and use was recognized and maintained through complex negotiations between the various si-yams of the numerous longhouses, and gatherings were coordinated by those who carried this responsibility to ensure the broadest possible engagement for discussion, negotiation, and agreement between the houses. No such process exists for those who would appropriate our stories. We never saw the land and its relatives as a source of wealth per se, but we were always aware of territoriality, the limits and extant of sharing between us. For example, Snauq'w was our garden, not just one village's garden, but a garden for all of the *Friendly* nations that had access to it.

Further, we were severally responsible for it. Laws and customs during harvest were practiced to ensure its continuance as a garden. Jurisdiction over the land was seen as much for the domain of caretaking responsibilities as our sustenance, while our art (carvings, blankets, stories, and songs) were seen as private or family property, and hence personal wealth, which was intended for giveaway. No wealth existed simply for its acquisition.

On the west coast, Coast Salish people interacted with all those living within the jurisdiction now known as Western Montana (Flathead Salish Territory), Southern BC, Vancouver Island, Washington State, and Northern Oregon. Each family developed knowledge through their interaction with one another, the land and the sea and all the beings in it, and they exchanged or shared it with others within this territory. Some families never stopped this practice. Geographical confluence with other villages, land-specific and ocean-specific learning occurred, and each family became known for their specific knowledge and carried the responsibility for maintaining the expertise they inherited from the learning of their si-yams, who then were responsible for caretaking the learning and transmitting it to their children. The learning, while collaborative, was kept and transmitted by the si-yams.

I am interested in reclaiming and rebuilding the systems

that existed prior to the arrival of a handful of powerful European men on our shores. I say a handful of powerful European men because the initial theft was conducted by white men, and it was maintained on behalf of the institutions they set into motion. That was how it happened. I am cognizant that non-Europeans (Asian, Black, and South American) and many Europeans (Irish, Ukrainians, etc.) came on different ships, with a lower level of theft entitlement. I am also interested in establishing a sharing arrangement between us that is fair for all of us. Like the late Art Manuel, I am not happy with the current arrangement (Art, son of George and Marceline Manuel—two of our previous leaders—has recently passed away. He was a constitutional lawyer, youth organizer, Red Power advocate, and founder of the Defenders of the Land movement).

Today, we are buying back our knowledge. I say this only so that our youth who attend these institutions to study themselves can be aware that they need not be grateful for their education. They stole our knowledge and are now selling it back to us. I believe this to be shameless, but it seems I am one of the few. Our youth need to know the extent of the pillaging of Indigenous knowledge and they need to know that it continues. That is the nature of capitalism, it continues to pillage.

I am also interested in memory, as our people did not write things down but developed a system of remembering who was responsible for what, who had access to what, how things were transmitted and earned, and what was available to all. This system identified the relationship of a person to family (house), clan (village), the clan to the nation or confederacy, if you will, and individuals were trained to remember in accordance with their natural bent toward subject. The relationship to land, trees, animals, fishes, etc., were part of the system we lived by. We understood these relationships and the expertise that each family contributed to the whole; it set into motion the visitations between villages and the discourse of the si-yams in the national life of the *confederacy*.

Residential school separated us from that understanding of our national systems, and during our absence Canada established many borders that would serve their increasing privilege and theft entitlement, while each of our villages became separated village from village, and our families were destroyed as school separated children from parents and parents from children and family from family. All of these separations facilitated further theft engagement and invasion and continue to do so. Tsawwassen was once connected to the whole; now it has made a real estate deal with the BC government outside of the whole.

In European law, oral knowledge is folk knowledge and so belongs to the public, which rationalizes the theft of our national intellectual knowledge base and privileges the written word as the only knowledge that is protected. Hence the education of children is biased toward reading and writing rather than remembering. While the written word is no more reliable than the remembered word, writing is privileged as "source documents," and memory is demeaned as unreliable because the European education system did not invent ways to cultivate reliable rememberers and so does not have a component in its education system that would teach children to become rememberers; it is not recognized as a way of knowing—they have no way to study and cannot imagine educative processes that would lead to systematic skill-building in remembering.

Children are called here, so we owe them the best present possible. Children are our future, and the future belongs to them. The land we use is borrowed against our children's future. These are all common sayings or teachings that have survived the holocaust we endured, the process of colonization we were subjected to, and the consequent disconnection from knowledge and transmission systems, as well as the dismemberment of our nations, that colonialism has resulted in. These teachings form the philosophical foundations of our laws.

Cultural and knowledge transmission exists primarily for children. Without children, knowledge atrophies and stasis replaces the internal dynamics of interaction, cultural transmission, and knowledge development, which are necessary for the intellectual growth of a people. This stasis and atrophy persist to this day because while we protect our ownership of story, song, dance, knowledge, and so forth, we are just now beginning to realize that we must revive the system to use, share, and transmit these things within Coast Salish families and between families.

Our children have a birthright; it is access to and use of sustenance materials (both tangible and intangible) within and on their territories (Turtle Island). They are entitled to whatever sustenance the land can provide (and the knowledge attached to the land and its sustenance); whether or not the oppressive state that claims to govern it agrees to this birthright, it does not eradicate its existence. As parents and grandparents, we are responsible for securing children's access and dominion to the land and its material and non-material (knowledge) sustenance and insuring they inherit this birthright. We are then also responsible for the state of the land. That responsibility carries with it the transmission and protection of the knowledge that travels with and arises from the land. No one but our children are entitled to our knowledge, stories, law, teachings, science, or medicine. We are responsible no matter what the newcomers' narrow parameters of permission grant us.

This birthright is not wanton, lustful, hedonistic, or exploitative. Our law is clear—sustenance has a covenant: the least damage to land and waters and the least invasive means possible are to be deployed to protect our relations (land and beings) in securing our existence. *All our relations* refers to the earth and all its beings in relationship to us. Relation implies a loving, caring, sustaining covenant between beings. We cannot exploit our relatives for our hedonistic aggrandizement. And we cannot endanger the cultural legacy of oratory our children are entitled to, nor can we exact favours from them or insist they earn the right to learn—they are entitled to our whole knowledge. As Indigenous people, we have agreements with all beings on this island that form what today are known as contracts. Violation of these agreements has consequences, in law and in life, and these consequences affect us personally and socially.

This covenant makes the elders, parents, grandparents, uncles, aunties—the entire adult population, whether they have personal progeny or not—responsible for the cultural education and guidance of all the children within the nation. We are the caretakers for both the earth and all of the human children. This makes every single adult a responsive Indigenous educator, regardless of whether we know enough to transmit the foundational knowledge required. The point is that all First Nations children are entitled to the entire body of knowledge of their nation, and the adults of the nation must see transmitting knowledge and culture as an imperative personal responsibility. This means we must acquire our knowledge if we don't have it, and if we do we *must* transmit it to our children.

Our children are in crisis. We all are aware of the burgeoning suicide among our youth. This is not the time to effect rules, regulations, and protocols on our youth's ability to acquire our knowledge, our stories, our songs, dances, and languages. Protocols are for outsiders. Our children are the only "insiders" in our nation. They are the only ones for whom culture exists. Cultural protocols exist for Outsiders who seek to learn from us. Outsiders know this. They also know they are asking for the birthright of our children.

Protection is from outside in. We need to protect our cultures from theft and misuse, from abuse and exploitation, but we do not necessarily need to adopt Western (private property–based) frameworks to do that. Right now we are teaching our young that they must conduct themselves in a certain way to access their knowledge (such as bringing tobacco, exacting favours, creating "helper status," which is tantamount to slavery). In the past, if someone wanted to excel at something, they apprenticed with a master. That was our *only* systemic means of transmission. While they were apprenticing, their families fed them. That is not the case today. We live in nuclear families and can hardly wait for our children to become adults so they will leave. We have schools our children attend. This means that adults who wish to access knowledge (after receiving the wrong education) must become an apprentice (without pay) to a master, and the apprentice may or may not be recognized as a master later. Further, the elder must agree to teach the incumbent student, generally without pay. This would not have been the case centuries ago.

We were once free, and in the course of our lives our children learned from us as they wished, they were our witnesses, our students, and they were around us all the time. They were expected to be curious, to learn, to query, and as adults, parents, grandparents, aunties and uncles, we constantly divulged and transmitted knowledge to them. Children were not required to tobacco their elders in the ordinary course of everyday living. Visitors who were adults and were not directly members of a specific family tobaccoed an elder in seeking specialized knowledge to which they were not normally entitled. This tells me that outsiders were not automatically entitled to our knowledge. In the past, at gatherings of clans from all over the territory, learned men and women would engage in discussion, and ceremonies always opened the discussions; tobacco was exchanged to ensure the good mind and knowledge were shared. The exchange was considered important to the well-being of the nation (confederacy) and so involved tobacco, but on ordinary summer days, as children walked with their grandparents, knowledge was exchanged without acknowledgement of tobacco. Children were not expected to gift their grandmother or grandfather for it; the knowledge was considered essential to transmit, and the child's birthright. I teach my grandchildren every chance I get, but do not expect tobacco for that. The tobacco requirement puts the child "outside my family," and I tend to think that Indigenous children in crisis are inside my sphere of grandmothering. Likewise, during the winter dances, ceremony was a part of the process of dancing, storytelling, and knowledge transmission, as outsiders became "insiders." We were not required to tobacco or gift our elders in this circumstance. In fact, those holding the ceremony gifted the visitors.

The exploitation of our people, the land, and its wealth, accompanied by the separation of our elders from their children during the residential school period, has created a situation in our communities in which our children are outsiders. We as elders are disconnected from our responsibility, and some of us are disconnected from our children. We must reconnect.

This is where the issue of appropriation of culture comes into play. We want our sensibility about ownership honoured by the Outsiders and we also want our children to pick up their cultural bundles and access their birthright. These two things are not the same. Our children will become sharing, caring, and responsive adults only if we are sharing, caring, responsive parents and teachers. Even when a story belonged to another family, members of that family were happy to share it, even if they were not with First Nations people from the same nation. As a child, I heard teachings, stories, and songs, witnessed dances, ceremonies, from non-family, from non-clan, non–First Nations people, and I always felt entitled to use those teachings, stories, songs, dances, and ceremonies. The elders made me feel like I belonged and so transmitted what I needed to know to be able to become the sort of elder who understood that children belong, they do not have to earn their access to the culture, the land, its sustenance, or our knowledge.

Protocols have come into being as a result of the desire of non-Indigenous people who no longer wish to appropriate knowledge or engage Indigenous people from a theft perspective and so are approaching Indigenous people for a way to connect. Their desire is to learn from our stories and our knowledge. Indigenous people are developing protocols to allow for this engagement while at the same time they are protecting their children's inheritance. These protocols protect our children's future. When a college or university employs us to divulge knowledge, which they then claim to own, because they caused it to develop or paid for its research, they are free to resell that knowledge to our children in perpetuity. This is not a responsive way to transmit knowledge to our children. We must continue to own the knowledge after the course, research, or knowledge has been developed.

The exploitative system that has replaced our systems has led us to protectionist policies that require our attention. It is theft and exploitation by foreigners when a university opts to jointly develop a course for which they own copyright of material in which even one of us was a participant. All our knowledge belongs to all of our grandchildren far into the future, whether that knowledge is art-based, philosophy-based, or story-based; we are merely the keepers of the knowledge for future generations. To sell our knowledge to someone who will charge our children tuition to acquire it is to violate our law.

Our cultural systems and the knowledge that holds them up must be recognized by the newcomers as a particular Indigenous nation's intellectual property that belongs to its children. Just as visitors from other communities within our nations had to respect our villages, we need the outsiders to respect our ways, our laws, and our sense of ownership. This begins with recognition. Recognition of the way we use and own song, dance, ceremony, and story, and how we keep these things in their original form and keep them in the family, cite their use and their origin, and how we share them with others. The oral presentations made in ceremony, the stories transmitted, the history transmitted, the knowledge transmitted orally, are kept by certain individuals in the families who are charged with the responsibility of caretaking and monitoring, determining their use and transmission. These keepers are responsible for transmitting the knowledge and cultural property specific to their families and protecting its original authority and authenticity. Since the outsiders have shown themselves to be engaged in exploitative relations with the land, it is incumbent upon us to ensure they are prepared to enter into a non-exploitative covenant with us and with the land and our knowledge. That is where ceremony and tobacco and gift exchange come into play. It is also where safeguarding our knowledge, customs, stories, songs, and dances comes into play.

A keeper of knowledge or story is a position of authority recognized by the community as the owner of certain knowledge, stories, laws, teachings, science, and medicine. The knowledge belongs to the family, and the family ensures that every generation a si-yam is educated to maintain the knowledge the family is responsible for keeping safe. That is, they are responsible for the origin of the story, song, and dance, the ceremony they keep alive and transmit to the children on behalf of the nation. They are responsible for its transmission and its good use. If we keepers are responsible for keeping knowledge and we pass it on to someone who is irresponsible, disrespectful, and exploitative, it is we who are responsible for their misuse. Sometimes it is our own children who, in their lack of familiarity with the law, practice misuse. This has happened many, many times to us, and so we are cautious.

We then feel forced to develop protocols to protect our knowledge and our cultures from misuse and abuse. This means that when we say, "Do not write this story down," it means that if you hear it, you may repeat it, providing you cite the source, but you cannot turn it to profit by writing it down and gaining royalties from it as though it were yours. If we explain that this story we are about to tell was told to young people during the transition from childhood to adulthood, it means the story belongs to teenagers—it is not there for the personal aggrandizement of the adult hearing it, whether they are First Nations or not. No one may use their knowledge to self-puff, to brag, to withhold, to lord over others, or to shame youth. The listener does not have bragging rights, or the right to profit from the story, no matter what their nationality, nor is the listener entitled to take teenagers hostage, extract favours of service from them or shame them with their lack of knowing.

Our knowledge, stories, songs, and dances do not exist to validate us as Sto:lo, Ojibway, or any other nation or clan; they are not there to guarantee us a place in the world. They are there to engage the listener in establishing a relationship to the land and help us to build good relations between beings and the land. I encourage all my listeners to use my stories in that way, but they must cite their origins, as I do. Stories are our helpers; they lead us to right living, to the good mind, to relationship with one another and the land. Stories help us to be human. In that sense, they are an appeal to the human soul divine, to the spirit, and in this way are spiritual helpers. They cannot be property in the same way that Europeans view their written word. When the author, the conjurer, is making it up before you, this can change how the story is treated. We understood that everyone had their own song. A personal song was just that, a personal song—no one would sing someone else's personal song without permission.

When we make up a new story, of course that becomes the story of the conjurer (author in Euro-English), but if a knowledge keeper is attempting to educate us in our national, historical, philosophical, or legal point of view, then the story doesn't belong to the individual, but rather the version belongs to the family and the keeper is sharing it, as is their responsibility to the whole nation. Our sense of courtesy and respect and recognition for the singer/story keeper forbids us from using a story that does not belong to us, so we refrain from doing that. Likewise, when I make up a story, it is my story; when I make a knowledge discovery, it is my knowledge; however, it is never completely disconnected from original knowledge, and we backtrack the knowledge trail, cite the individuals who contributed to it, before we advance the thought.

Any Indigenous person may use my stories to springboard off and reconceive of the story and tell it back different but the same; that is, Indigenous people, particularly children, can reimagine the story, decipher what they believe is the message, and create a new one from the original teaching or message without violating copyright (in our minds). In this way, we join the story maker, the myth maker, in the creation of a new story. We are entitled to do this.

We are also entitled to build stories collaboratively. We do it all the time, sitting around the kitchen table—someone starts telling a story and we all add to it. We build story collectively, but we do not run off and get it published as our own, because it is oral, and all knowledge that is oral is folk knowledge and therefore belongs to the public. Anything else is unacceptable.

None of the above makes our stories, our songs, or our knowledge property in the Western sense, but they are like property. Our languages have names for songs, for stories, for knowledge—none of the words translate directly into *property*. We must use our own words, or translate them carefully. We want a non-exploitative relationship with the outsiders and we want that street to go two ways; that is, we want them to stop being exploitative in their relations with us. We wish them to stop appropriating the land's wealth, but this does not make the earth or this island a large piece of real estate or property. We are caretakers who must guard the knowledge, the stories, the songs, dances, art, and ceremonies of our na-tions, but this means we must be willing to transmit these stories, songs, and dances to our children and protect them from exploitation by those who would appropriate. When you give me tobacco, you are recognizing that you are asking for knowledge to which you are not entitled by birth.

For exploitation to exist, the item, the being, the spirit must be appropriated and turned to profit by the individual doing the appropriation. Western society believes that once written, knowledge, story, song, etc., become property, intellectual property, and they have copyright laws protecting it. They maintain that oral knowledge is not property—i.e., for it to become property, the individual must do something to it. We don't get this; we can't wrap our spiritual sensibility, our heart, or our mind around it. This reminds me of how the mink be-came small. He exploited the goodwill of bear, rabbit, and mouse women until bear squeezed him and squeezed him and he became a skinny little weasel. Which reminds me of the rationale for stealing the land: the Indian isn't doing anything with the land and so he is not entitled to it, and so they took it. We maintain that a farm is not necessarily an improvement on the land, while European law maintains it is an improvement. We maintain that we do not have to do anything to our stories to make them ours. Europeans maintain that we must write them down, transform them into metaphor. This notion of writing things down contains a kind of incarceration of story. A sentence is captured, rendered permanent, unchangeable, static, still, dead. I write only the fictional, today-versions of our story—in this way, I am working with the story, keeping it moving, fluid, alive, and ready for some other Sto:lo child to work with, play with, and continue to use it. Our stories exist; they have existed for thousands of years.

We as story keepers are responsible for ensuring that our children may access them for thousands of years forward without it costing them an arm and a leg, or the purchase of a course, the purchase of a book; hence, every time I engage Indigenous youth, I tell as many stories as I can. When I write stories down, I encourage Indigenous youth to use them, tell them back different but the same, so that a new generation of storytellers may be born. Likewise with medicine: someone wants to know what to do about warts, I tell them the milk from dandelion or milk thistle helps, and I encourage them to pass it on. They do. They tell others, "Lee Maracle says..." And so they pass it forward and our children are educated in this way, in our story and medicine, our teachings, so that they may be who they are and always will want to be (Len George teaching).

When I am speaking to Europeans, I have to explain the complexities of ownership and used to make sure they did not abuse or hoard or resell our stories. This is as much as I see. Someone else, younger than me, will have to add to this story, I have no more to say about it. Each generation adds its history of seeing to every story, and so we accumulate knowledge.

Not long ago, a Canadian asked if they could write stories with Indigenous characters in it if it was fiction. Of course you can, but why would you? You are taking space at the table that our writers need to earn their way as writers. Sharing space and time is the opposite of racism. Occupying another people's space and time is racism. Why can you not stop "fucking caribou squaws" or writing about "dirty half-breeds" (Al Purdy and Margaret Laurence).

Have we not had enough torment from Canadians?

Conversation II:
How does colonialism work?

One of the most complicated conversations I need to have with Canadians is about colonialism itself. In *Memory Serves*, I discussed colonialism in terms of viruses colonizing the body. Perhaps we are still that primal—or at least some people are, without a strong cultural foundation, and so can be completely colonized. I am often asked to speak about colonization and decolonization and I get the feeling that everyone thinks it is a mental exercise. A colony is a space—a physical space that once belonged to someone or something else: like tuberculosis colonizing the lung. It once belonged to the breather but now is occupied by the tubercular bacteria and the host will die of it if a war is not waged against the tuberculosis. It is not an idea that the host needs to rid themselves of the bacteria. An idea will not help save the patient. Likewise with decolonizing in general. You can decolonize your mind—if there is no space in your mind that allows for the expertise or superior knowledge of the colonized, then you need to create space for that thought, decolonize your mind—but that is not decolonization in general. Decolonization in general is to take back the land, space, territory and governance as well as the economy of your original country. (See *Memory Serves*.)

Teachers fall on your path and all you have to do is look for them. One such person for me is artist Susan Blight: once she unraveled some long-standing colonial confusion for me when she told an audience, "It is not about our knowledge fitting into yours—decolonization is about how you fit into us." I just wanted to bust up laughing, so simple and so complex and so true all at once. Her words served as an understatement for me.

Ms. Blight had spiraled to the center of a wheel of spokes and provided the point to which all the disordered spokes could anchor themselves. She had thus provided me with a wheel of understanding. I spent all day and half the night hooking the spokes to this center. It held so many of my spokes in place. I felt clear. This is our country. You were granted permission to live here and the conditions of that permission are embedded in treaties and recent court decisions. Nowhere in these treaties or court decisions does it say we grant you permission to take over management and control of our territories and our lives.

"But you don't own the land" is the answer I get from Canadians who immediately retreat to arguing in favour of colonial control of us and our territory to protect their invasion and right to super-exploit the land.

I have been thinking about that statement lately: but you don't own the land.

This strikes me as insidious. I mean, after all, you are the ultimate believers in private property and the faithful in the concept of Canada as *not* an Indigenous homeland. Canadians are also the only benefactors of the belief that we do not own the land. Everyone who has ever said this to me means that I am disinherited and someone else is the inheritor of my home-land. It reminds me of Thomas King, who says they use your own words to beat you up. What they don't realize is that our own words contain a totally different intention.

Conversation 12:
Response to empathy from settlers

Among the many comments settlers have made is to refer to Indigenous people as the most marginalized people in Canada. Marginalized from what? And from whom? To make this statement, the person must believe that colonialism is the final state of affairs and the best we can get is to leave our nations behind and participate fully in our colonization. Marginalization: in order for me to be marginalized in your mind, you must be further convinced that you are at the center of the universe.

Like other Indigenous people believe, I am standing at the center of my own wheel of relations. You can find a four-directions wheel by Lillian Pitawanakwat in which she shows this in a diagram. In the image she created, the circle is a sphere. She refers to it as "sacred knowledge." It articulates in visual form the connections of every individual to all other beings on earth and in the sky world—the galaxy. It places the individual in the center of the circle of humanity and humanity in the centre of the sky, water, and earth worlds. This teaches us our place in relation to everything.

It is also about our responsibility to all beings—earth, sky, and human. The earth is at the bottom "holding all of humanity up"; the sky is at the top, inviting us to our final resting place in the spirit world and reminding us of our beginning place. In the paintings of Alex Janvier (Cree), we can see the synapses of creation reaching out from the bottom—earth—and from the top—the sky world. Dr. Karyn Recollet (Cree, professor at University of Toronto in Women's Studies) and I were discussing this with artist-in-residence Amanda Black, and Karyn pointed out that "we don't often think about things reaching down to us. It is important to remember that we are reaching up and the sky is reaching down." This is an important Ojibway-Cree perception.

Because the earth is holding us up, it reminds us of our obligation to all the beings that sustain us, including the earth mother, who literally permits us to walk all over her. The sky is unending. It contains the bird world, the world of the dead, and "star nations," or the galaxy. The connections then are completely clear and endless. The possibilities are endless. The very endlessness of possibility is the source of inspiration, the dreaming world, the imagination, and our ability to recover from the trials of daily life. Picture the endless capacity for joy in making endless relations with all the beings in the universe. This is what is meant by the path.

To the Cree and Ojibway, the dreaming world is the important world. In Cherie Dimaline's (Metis) new book, *The Marrow Thieves*, non-Natives are hunting Indigenous people because they want their bone marrow. The non-Natives have lost the ability to dream and the Indigenous people have not, and they believe the ability to dream is in the marrow of the Indigenous people. While this is science fiction, it is plausible to us. Scientists have been stealing our DNA for decades now.

We sued them for it and lost the court case—the scientists changed the DNA and copyrighted it, which makes it not ours.

In our sensibility, stealing someone's DNA, altering it, and winning the court case is the ultimate in dishonesty. Canadian law accommodates dishonesty. Who can have faith in such a legal system? We can only surmise that the laws of Europeans are founded on principles of dishonest, meaningless relationships with others. Maybe this is why so many of them believe the economy is the foundation of everything. This leads to all kinds of fallacious thinking: career is more important than social responsibility, economic development is about jobs and is more important than the environment, etc. Canadians come before us and all humans come before plants, animals, stone, metal, oil, and so forth.

According to Alanna Mitchell in her book *Sea Sick: The Global Ocean in Crisis*, we are standing at the precipice of a mass extinction event. I think the tsunamis of late are part of the mass extinction events, as are the heat waves of some decades ago that killed hundreds of thousands of people globally. The hurricanes, too, are connected to our extinction. They are all warnings. Indigenous people have always believed that we are "good for nothing" when it comes to the earth. We are critical to no other life form. Even the man-eating crocodiles, eels, sharks, and hippos have other choices. The earth cannot do without bacteria, mosquitoes, bees, and other such small beings, but it can do without us and thrive. This should humble us. We should stop calling ourselves the top of the food chain, the top of the life forms. This anthropocentric narcissism costs us lives on this planet.

Rather than looking at where we are in the hierarchical order of things, we should look at our responsibility toward the lives we are dependent upon. In any relationship we have responsibilities, obligations, and disciplined interaction. We cannot simply do "whatever we want" in the name of freedom. We can benefit from wanting and engaging in relations with endless beings. The engagement of relationship with endless beings means there are endless possibilities and endless joy to be received from others, and there is endless joy to offer.

Our freedom can be found only through the joy of relationship-building, the call out to the earth, its living beings, and the joy of receiving the support we need and the joy of carrying out our responsibilities to all. Children understand this. They have just left the spirit world and know something about the magic of earth. They run about, learning from bugs and animals and collecting stones as though they were sacred, no matter what race they are. Indigenous people encourage these beliefs and practices of toddlers, while education destroys it.

All humans who are alive are being held up in this way. All engagement is a moment of sharing, every morsel of food a moment of sharing from earth to us and back. This engagement addresses the aloneness that all humans feel and many of us fear. It appeases our sense of "just me," which is the seat of greed.

The four cardinal points begin in the east and end in the north, representing four directions. The seven stages of life are also found on this four-directions wheel. They begin in the east and move across the wheel to the west, ending in the north. The good life or, for Salish people, *the good mind/ heart*, teaches the adult world their responsibility to children and requires that we provide absolute goodwill toward them. This goodwill is critical to becoming a person who is honest, humble, courageous, wise, respectful, generous, and loving.

Lovingness is not about the sort of courtesy that Canadians practice as the nice people of the world. Loving requires a strategic commitment to continuously share and nurture that which you are dependent upon—first the water, then earth, then the sky, then the beings of these worlds, and finally all humans. Our food, clothing, etc., comes from Third World countries, so if anything, they deserve at the minimum our respect. Instead we invite them here to engage first-hand our disrespect.

The fast life: teenagehood.

The wandering life, picking up knowledge, experiences, testing out theories—this is the work of the wandering life. Filling our baskets with knowing, studying phenomena, engaging in relationships, failing, learning from our failures, re-evaluating ourselves, and beginning anew. These are important parts of becoming a person who has discovered what truth is, the necessity for planning, and testing the vitality of executing a plan. Cumulatively, if the child lives this life, they become what is regarded as an "elder" or a si-yam, someone who has knowledge.

Humility is critical to recognizing and examining our failures, our mistakes, our contribution to broken relations, and the origins of dropping our bundles, neglecting our relations, ignoring our obligations, and the emptiness that creates. Courage gives us the determination to overcome our fear of self-examination, of admitting to our neglect. Honesty teaches us to own our self, our emotionality, our thoughts, our desires, and our very path. Face ourselves. Respect, generosity, and love guide our path to relationship.

These are the seven teachings within each direction of the wheel, and there are subsets within each of those seven teachings. The origins of medicines and what they mean is a subset of a teaching. Thus the wheel becomes a mnemonic device for remembering. It also structures the relationship between one teaching and another, and our relationship to the teaching.

I have laws, I have politics, I have beliefs, I have story. What I don't have is access to my land—someone else is preventing me to access my land by dint of the bayonet and maintains it by a host of laws that are enforced by your hired guns (police and army). Do not mistake my kindness in not responding to your hired guns for a deluded belief in your centrality. Do not mistake my kindness for acceptance of the absence of the right of access to my land or for the absence of my love for it. Further, do not mistake my kindness for a relinquishment of who I am and who I will always want to be.

Settlers ought to look at their history, then look in the mirror. After annihilating our populations, and much of the animal life on this continent and in the oceans, and after spoiling the air, the lands, and the waters, who would want to be you?

Conversation 13:
Reconciliation and residential school as an assimilation program

On June 1, 2008, the Truth and Reconciliation Commission was established to examine the residential school system. The commission completed its inquiry in December 2015, and although its work is not over yet, its offices officially closed. In the course of its work, the commission clearly described residential school as an act of cultural genocide, yet Indigenous scholars and political leaders and Canadian government officials are referring to it as an assimilation program. So many Canadians are asking me about reconciliation.

This is a bit of a misnomer, as the conciliation of the reconciliation is unknown to many Indigenous people. In fact, Charlie Jones, a Nuu-Chah-Nulth elder who lived well past one hundred, talked about being murdered by holy men with small-pox blankets. How anyone could refer to this as conciliatory is beyond me, but it is one of the myths Canada and its population hold up. Canada views itself as the nicest colonizer in the world. It does not ask the colonized if they agree with this, Canadians just keep repeating it to each other like bobbleheads that can't stop bobbling. It doesn't occur to them that this statement requires our agreement to be true.

Canada is steeped in this sort of mythological madness, which was the foundation of forming the policy of residential school. Like Tom Fitzgerald and Lorenzo Marquez's book *Everyone Wants to Be Me or Do Me: Tom and Lorenzo's Fabulous and Opinionated Guide to Celebrity Life and Style*, colonial policymakers believe we all want to be them. Then they conjured the myth of civilization and set to build residential schools so that we *could* become them. Or so the story goes. Problem was, the truth is a long way from this myth.

In the first fifty years, thousands of children died. In 1907, Dr. Peter Henderson Bryce, the medical inspector to the Department of the Interior and Indian Affairs, discovered that 50 per cent of the children died in residential school. When he complained to the superintendent of Indian Affairs that the children in residential school were dying of disease, the superintendent responded: "If they are dying, isn't that the point?"

To then refer to these schools as assimilation programs is another Canadian psychotic lie. We ought not to repeat that lie. To experiment with three thousand children by starving them and then monitoring the effect on their starvation is an act of genocide no less serious than those experiments the Nazis performed on Jewish children.

Residential school was a genocide program. Below is Article 2 of the United Nations Genocide Convention, signed by Canada in December 1948 and ratified on September 12, 1952:

ARTICLE 2

In the present convention, genocide means any of the following acts committed with intent to destroy, in whole or in part, a national, ethnic or religious group as such:

a) Killing members of the group [thousands of Indigenous children died without treatment and several thousands more were starved as an experiment];

b) Causing serious bodily or mental harm to members of the group [thousands were harmed in every possible way imaginable];

c) Deliberately inflicting on the group conditions of life calculated to bring about its physical destruction in whole or in part [hunger, deprivation, murder of food sources, banning of procurement of food, plunder of resources for someone else's benefit, and continuing to remove our children from our care all have led to our destruction];

d) Imposing measures intended to prevent births within the group [the eugenics laws, involuntary and coerced sterilization];

e) Forcibly transferring children of the group to another group [residential school and continued child apprehension and removal].

Anyone who thinks this is over because we had the Commission of Inquiry is doubly deluded.

The uninvestigated murder of Indigenous women and the failure of the state to even establish an inquiry until September 2016 into why it continues is genocide as well. The removal continues as adoption, child apprehension, and the fostering out of our children has surpassed the removal of children for residential school education. It is a continuous violation of Article 2b) causing bodily or mental harm, and 2e) forcibly transferring children of the group to another group. Refusing medical parity on and off reserve, isolation, and plundering our land resources gratuitously violates Article 2c. And lastly, the eugenics laws that sterilized thousands of Indigenous people (particularly women) while their children languished in residential schools is yet another violation of the genocide convention. The above is not over.

Removal was the object of residential school, and it was not for purposes of assimilation, and it was a crime. It was done to destroy the language, culture, and sensibility of Indigenous people. This is genocide. No academic or English language or mathematics or science courses were taught in the first one hundred years of those schools. Those would be the sort of courses that would justify calling it an assimilation program. Instead only the destruction of Indigenous language and knowledge was offered. Children worked and recited scripture when they were not being beaten, starved, or raped. When are rape and hunger part of an assimilation program? Only when it applies to us. Elsewhere in the world, it is genocide.

"Complicity in genocide" is genocide: Article 3e. Those who gain land and wealth from the conquest theft of another people's country or property are complicit. Canadians happily receive billions of dollars in wealth from our territories without our permission or agreement and without payment whatsoever, while we are continuously subjected to genocide programs of one sort and another. This makes Canadian settlers complicit in the plunder.

Whose wealth do you think you are thriving on? This is not Europe, this is not Africa, and this is not Asia. Where do you think this is?

Question: "What is reconciliation to you?"

Someone asked me this after I gave a presentation on the Missing and Murdered Indigenous Women and Girls. I thought he was being sarcastic or else the question was just asinine. Did he know the meaning of the word *reconciliation*? I could not believe he had jumped to this conclusion without considering that the killing was not over. Did he think we were friends before those men killed us? Did he think we liked them before they killed us? Did he think I was their friend when they killed those other women?

"Well, stop killing us would be a good place to begin," I answered. The audience laughed. "Then maybe stop plundering our resources, stop robbing us of our children, end colonial domination—return our lands, and then we can talk about being friends. I can't believe we are having this conversation after you listened to my presentation about the murder of Indigenous women and children. It is embarrassing—not for me, but for you." We stared at each other for a long time.

As I look at him, I think this person in front of me is struggling with my very humanity. I believe this is the first time in his life any Indigenous woman ever challenged Canada's right to oppress us. He does not seem to get that we are human beings and we do not deserve what we are receiving from his country. At the end of the reading, he buys several books. Clearly he realized he needed to know something.

I always take the time out to write something when I am asked to present and rarely use the written material to actually make the presentation. But just in case, I am jotting down some remarks as I believe this is a very auspicious occasion, and I want to make sure I don't miss any points. This is the first ever First Nations Literature conference held by India. Such an important occasion deserves my best attention.

All former colonies of England struggle with reconciling with the colonial terminology that continues to dominate education on a global scale. It occurs to me that simply calling written story "literature," as the colonial authorities do, and establishing a definition of what makes good story and what doesn't, and creating a structure around who gets to redefine what story is, creates a near impossible conundrum for First Nations people. English literature experts are all those people who have passed through the gates established by the official British gatekeepers who have assigned themselves, and themselves alone, the authority to name what is art and what is not art, what is literature and what is not literature.

First Nations people were declared the very antithesis of culture, art, and morality when Europe colonized the world. There are a number of ironies in this. Modern literature is born of the cultural engagement of non-Indigenous people and the colonial settlers.

First, the so-called father of modern literature in North America is Ralph Waldo Emerson. Mr. Emerson was a self-proclaimed Indigenist anarchist—that is, he ascribed to the oratorical teachings of Indigenous people and their system of governance. Even as the state was killing us, declaring us vanishing and defiling every aspect of our culture, art, and morality, we were influencing the direction of modern literature through the Indigenist writers of whom Emerson was a key figure and the greatest influence on the direction of literature in modern times.

Emerson's ascription to Indigenous thought and orality, however, did not keep us safe. His defense of us did not elevate our word art to an equal position in Western society because it was "Not Written." To be literature, the story has to first be written. This is the conundrum. I want to coin a new term: Word Art, which encompasses all art formed by using words: hip-hop, folk poetry, spoken word, orality, storytelling, and so forth.

All the settlers of America, Mexico, and Canada had to do was keep us from writing to secure first place in the world of literature. In the case of the Aztecs and Mayans, the Spanish had to destroy their writing and stop them from continuing to write. Two hundred years later, we are gathered in India to talk about First Nations Literature. Again, the irony is not lost on me.

I want to say that the influence of our societies on Western society went far beyond mere story. It extended to science, medicine, democracy, politics, and law—human rights and acceptance of homosexuality. We were called savages, not because we were brutal in any way. The Jesuits referred to our dress code (women showing skin), our sexuality (women were permitted to be permissive, as it were; homosexuality was accepted), and our polity (women had equal authority to men). Two hundred years later these practices are accepted in the US and Canada and a number of other countries globally. We have influenced the world, but no one has to credit us, as there is no written document by the settler to vouchsafe that fact—in fact, there is, but no one is seriously looking for it.

It is only recently that we have English literary scholars, but they aren't seriously looking for the connection between modern literature and our oratorical influence either. Perhaps they don't have the oratorical history of colonialism that I inherited. Our orality is not simply about our stories. It is about our sociology, our science, our horticulture, aqua culture, our medicine, our law, our politics, and, lastly, our story. The stories were essentially for children. Stories were our transmission system for educating our children in the law, politics, medicine, and traditions of the nation. Stories that have been translated by Western anthropologists contain gendered pronouns, something many of our languages do not have. Many elders dealt with English pronouns in a number of ways; first, some would say "she" if the teller was a woman, or "he" if the teller was a man. Since most of the time the anthropologists' informants were men, Raven comes off as a "he." Raven is Raven; there is no "he" or "she" when we speak of raven.

When I first wrote my novel *Ravensong*, the white male critics castigated it as "containing too much" that is outside the realm of orthodox literature, i.e., there is medical knowledge, sociology, politics, and power in the story and no protagonist/

antagonist fight per se, though the old snake, some would, say fulfills that role. He was not intended to. The story is about Stacey crossing the bridge and attending university in white town. Things happen during the summer she was to leave. Stacey is a full participant in her life. She is a Sto:lo woman. Anything that happens in her village is her life.

I pointed out to the world at the time that I believed that fiction was about painting and freedom. People argued with me until I told them that these were not my words, but the words of an accepted literary figure in their tradition, Henry James. Finding a European icon to persuade others of the validity of our theoretical perceptions of story is humiliating at best, colonized at worst, but it is what we have to do to be heard. White men, particularly old, dead, white writers, hold a monopoly on what story/fiction is all about.

Our lives were and still are deep and complicated morasses of law, politics, medicine, sociology, and power. Naturally, our stories reflect that. White folks have my country, my body as an uneducated savage, and I must find a white guy or gal to validate my thoughts if I am to be believed. This was true until other people of colour began to write. Many believe me when I articulate the forgoing; now white Canadians feel obligated to listen.

The work of the artist is to ensure that this is storied up and not harangued upon. I challenged the critics to cite the harangues, to cite the didacticism in my work—no one could. One of the critics gave it a more thorough read and admitted to being dismissive in his initial critique. Dismissive. That is our history with colonial settlers.

We do not control the gates. We are not entitled to educate anyone but ourselves, and the subject must be ourselves. We are there to be educated and they are quite clear about that.

We are educated by them in order to stand at the gate and beg to be let in. Because we are educated by them, we tend to look at the things they want to see, rather than looking at things from our orality's point of view. Some people are trying to elevate orality to the level of literature. I wonder why this is necessary. There never was a hierarchy in my mind. Our word art is as valuable, as elegant, as rich, as artful as anything that they have managed to come up with, they just don't see it that way. I wonder sometimes if we do.

A story is word art, whether it is told, performed, written, or dramatized—it is all word art. This is the only expression that erases the conundrum, makes us equal, and eradicates the privilege of the Euro-Western paradigm. I wonder if we are terrified of doing that. I am a gifted word artist. When I recite a poem, people are moved. When I tell a story, people are moved. When I read a story, people are moved. That makes me a dramatic, spoken, and written word artist. I take an old story and I recraft it as a novel. I work with it and work with it until it sings like the original story I am working with. I work with it and work with it until our world is omnipresent in the story. What they don't see is that their stories do the same thing. There is no story without law, politics, power, and sociology worth telling.

I remember my Ta'ah asking me to read to her. I picked Dickens's *A Christmas Carol* and I read it the way I was taught. She grumped that I must not be reading it right, because it didn't sound any good. I went home that night and reread that story until I could perform it. I am so grateful for that, as I could not perform it until I really understood it. The next day I went back and jumped up and dramatized the story. When I finished, she told me the story of the double-headed serpent and the boy who saved our villages by making a deal with the serpent and bringing our people back to a good mind. When she finished, she said, "It's the same story everywhere, I guess."

I once learned a song: "Inky Dinky Spider." I sang it to her. She didn't think I was singing it right. When I went home, I had to ask my dad what a "water spout" was, and he told me. I went back the next day and reworked the story into a clear bit of drama for myself. While singing, I watched the whole story. Children need to dramatize story to understand it.

This worked well when I had to "read to my children." I dramatized Shakespeare, Dickens, Farley Mowat, and Jack London, and a number of American classics for them. I came to understand Europeans and their art. There is as much law, politics, and sociology in their stories as there is in mine, but they agree with their own polity, legal system, and sociological structures, whereas they are not all that interested in mine—it twangs their guilt. However, given the global mess we are all in, with poverty marking our lives the way it does, with the destruction of the environment heading the world pell-mell for a mass extinction event, the world needs our story. It needs modern novels born of old story. It needs drama born of old story. It needs music born of old story.

A major book publisher solicited a manuscript from me and, after looking at it, dismissed it as "too ethnic." I made it more ethnic and found another publisher—the first publisher needs to be pissed off a little.

I was on tour with Dionne Brand, Nicole Brossard, and Barbara Gowdy in England in 1992. Despite the fact that Thomas King had released *Medicine River*, I was the only Indigenous writer that England considered literary. That, of course, was before the feminists got hold of Tom King's work and lauded it to the skies. I thought it rather snooty of them to make this judgment on the one hand, and rather non-feminist of

Canadian self-declared feminist authors to focus on the promotion of Native male writing, though when I think of the era in which I was publishing, it is not surprising. The feminist movement has the dubious honour of having advocated the support of "women" *and* Native people—i.e., the AFN and chiefs' organizations—as though there were no women among us.

All that was going on before the work of the likes of Marilyn Dumont, Louise Bernice Halfe, and Eden Robinson came along. There are a number of writers since who have elevated writing to the literary level besides the foregoing: Joanne Arnott, Cherie Dimaline, and Columpa Bobb. Although these women have been writing for almost two decades now, the focus is still on men. At a recent literary conference in Canada, Marilyn Dumont said, "If you are a woman writer, you will have a hard time." I want to leave out Eden Robinson, not because she deserves my lack of attention, but because she writes in a genre with which I am unfamiliar, Gothic fiction, but I can't. I want to say that I am not a fan of Gothic anything, but I definitely support Robinson's work and choice of genre. We have two inheritances as Indigenous people, our own and the one forced upon us.

Someone once asked me if I speak my own language. I had been speaking for an hour. I seethed out, "This is my language, I earned it, my people died for it, they bled for it, they grieved for the loss of their children for it—it is mine. Did you earn it the same way I did?" We write in it. Every genre, every style, every technique, whether an Indigenous or Eurocentric literary technique, was earned and offered, and we are entitled to it. It cost us a continent. We have paid for it. This is true for all Indigenous people. Our stories come from our two threads of history.

I am most familiar with my own thread. So when I read Marilyn Dumont's "A Letter to Sir John A. Macdonald," I am more than simply amused. First, she is addressing a dead prime minister who Canada accolades as the "founder of Canada" and who is despised by many Metis, my mother included, many Scot nationalists, Irish, and many Indigenous people of Manitoba and elsewhere as a cad—a drunken cad who destroyed three groups of people's dreams. A "Dear John letter" is a Canadian cultural phenomenon that a woman writes to a man with whom she has a relation that she wishes to end. And Marilyn is such a woman and she ends the relation. Marilyn is Metis, this is her culture, but she is also Indigenous, so when she talks about these "long cabin syllables of colonialism," how they did not work, that she is still here and Metis, she is coming from her Indigenous cross-pollinated roots. (I know she did not write the foregoing. The exact quote is: "Cabin syllables / Nouns of settlement, / ...steel syntax [and] / The long sentence of its exploitation"; the "long cabin syllables" is a springboard from her work. In Western thinking, there is no room for the courtesy I am extending Marilyn in putting my thoughts in quotes. They are directly from her, so I quote her. I would not have that thought were it not for her words. Sto:lo courtesy requires that I learned this: long cabin syllables of colonialism, from Marilyn Dumont. Western courtesy does not require it.)

In this work, Marilyn braids the sensibility of all three cultures that objected to McDonald's colonial expansion—the Scot nationalists, the Cree people, and the Metis—and she does so with brilliance and alacrity—very tribal. Dumont does so as a "Dear John letter," which becomes a double humiliation for Sir John. First, because Indigenous women sit below women in general, and women in general are definitely out of the sightline of Sir John. At the time, white women were chattel, the property of white men. So Dumont's "we are still here and half breed" has a layered textual meaning that becomes comic in an Indigenous and tribal sense.

Sir John is upbraided by a woman—not just any woman, but the half-breed woman he was trying to annihilate. Sir John lost further: it is an Indigenous woman who points out that the project was doomed to failure, as the French were never committed to it, and this is her heritage too. In fact, Quebec supported Riel so much so that Sir John said, "Louis Riel will hang though every dog in Quebec barks." Dumont is thumbing her nose at the longevity of Canada as compared to hers.

And lastly, unlike over one hundred years ago, women, specifically half-breed women, have a voice and a very good memory and they write—well. The poem is comic, unless you are Sir John, then it is tragic. Throughout the text, the reader is reminded of the darker side of Sir John, wishing the Metis dead, so being a fan of his is difficult. With her layered text, clarity of purpose, and sure voice, Marilyn reminds us we belong here, we have a place here and no one can take that away.

Louise Halfe, another one of my favourite feminist Indigenous poets, has two threads to her history; on the one hand she is Cree, but she has Metis roots as well. In one of her poems, she writes that her grandmother told her "not to step over a man when you are on your moon time, you will rob him of his power." "Funny," she answers, "I thought that was the point." In these two lines, she sums up our current historical condition, with humour and grace.

First, we are no longer the authors of the destiny of our nations. Patriarchy has invaded our community. We are lesser than, and so to be Cree, to be Metis, to be Salish, we must assume our authority, our place. If someone has greater authority by reason of their gender, all bets are off. That is, we need to restructure ourselves in such a way that we are able to take our place. Accommodating those with greater entitlement is the opposite of what needs to happen. We need to learn to share equal space and time with women. Layered text. The Indigenous women authors do it best; Western European literary critics cannot deal with layered text, but we can and we do.

Cherie Dimaline in *Red Rooms* creates a whole new way of telling a series of interconnected short stories about people who are disconnected. This is the work of women, to reconnect the disconnected. This is our job, and Cherie is familiar with it. This was our role and the seat of our authority in our community. Cherie picks up the thread of her authority in *Red Rooms*, comically, dramatically, and beautifully. The people in the rooms are among those who are passing into the spirit world, and so the storyteller strives to make their lives significant and worthy of community retelling. Her narrator is a seer; no one else in "Indian country" besides myself chooses to bring this gift forward, and I did so with little courage compared to the Ravenesque cheek and brass that Ms. Dimaline exhibits in *Red Rooms*.

When I first read the work, I was embarrassed for my stingy treatment of Celia, the seer in *Ravensong*. Dimaline covers all aspects of the need to change our attitudes toward homosexuals, abused women, alienated men, and our fractured community. She does it with humour, serious narration, and great wit. And she does so by connecting the seer to the community of the dying. She does so as a Metis, for both Treaty and the Metis, just as Riel did. Riel included everyone: Scots who are white, French who are white, and the Metis and Indigenous people. That was the magic and magnificence of the Manitoba Metis struggle.

Columpa Bobb is a playwright who believes every subject is up for grabs. She dares to turn Euro children's songs into adult plays, traditional story into children's plays, and she dares to co-write with European playwrights to create a show that functions as both great children's and adult theatre. In her work *Wings of Darkness*, she takes the Bat Story (a Salish traditional story) and transforms it into a modern play focused on the problem of gangs among Canada's Indigenous youth. In *Jumping Mouse*, she, along with her co-writer, Marion de Vries, mounts the story of how mouse became an eagle. In *Dinky*, she deals with the subject of death and the theme of grit and determination. She does so from two strands of her history, the theatrical tradition of the Salish people and the European tradition of playwriting. She does this as a woman, an advocate of justice, and as an individual who sees Indigenous people from a non-stereotypical view. Her partner and co-writer for *Jumping Mouse* holds the same view. Again, she brings the phenomenon of layered, brilliant wordplay and the cultural continuity of the place of women in Indigenous society and the future place of all women.

This is the foundation of Dalit: respect for women, the centrality of women, and the brilliance of layered text, wordplay, and drama, which will lead us to good relations, equitable sharing arrangements between men and women. I love history as much as the next person, but I cannot love the displacement of women. Our societies were sharing societies; no one was left out. In the stories and poetry and plays of the above, there is an insistence on sharing space and time. I cannot participate in any gathering in which women are not accorded the space and time to present by those who would elevate a man to a greater space and a greater amount of time. This is true for me as an artist and as a si-yam of my people.

We have done enough voyeuristic looking at what white men did to us. We need to gather up our cultural bundles, organize our youth to seek out the stories we know are there in our oral repertoire, and put them to the page. We need to ensure that in so doing, our young women have a place. I do that wherever I am, wherever I go, and whenever I read, write, or witness theatre. I will not apologize for that.

Our knowledge keepers were trained to be rememberers. They were educated to recall the significant in what is said or done. Others, thinkers, were trained to examine the action and assure that the direction the nation took in responding to an event did not lead to a divergence from the original path. Indigenous leaders and thinkers accounted to community, clan, and nation in determining what actions to take in response to whatever change the nation faced. The confederacies responded to change as a part of life.

Young people are called upon to fill their baskets, to create life, to transform life, to engage the world and the community in this creative process. Penny Couchie, the co-artistic director of Aanmitaagzi, understands this and has spent twenty years of her artistic life doing this. As has her husband, Sid Bobb, co-artistic director of Aanmitaagzi. My first deep impression of her work was as part of the *Agua* production at Harbourfront many years ago with Alejandro Nuñez. I wrote my impressions immediately after watching their show.

I include this writing as a way of responding to the many questions I get about art creation and community. My daughter Columpa Bobb also created community art with children while empowering them to become good citizens. In so doing, she created a techno-stage set (she could not afford a set designer due to cutbacks) and engaged her students in the creation of their technology-driven set. She also developed a backbone for a play that can be changed and remounted, depending on the community that gets involved.

Columpa has influenced and trained many theatre people in her lifetime—including Sid and Penny of Aanmitaagzi. So the following is also a tribute to her:

Like everyone else at Harbourfront, I waited with curious and anxious anticipation for Earth in Motion's dance, *Agua/Water*, to begin. While we fidgeted, young men and women were carefully placing lit candles in the pond under the cover of a cool Toronto night sky. I knew of Alejandro Nuñez in the same way that many First Nations people had heard of the choreographer. I knew Penny Couchie as the love of my son's life. Both Couchie and Alejandro had developed this dance showpiece as their dance company's first production. I expected wonder, innovation, and beauty. What I received was magic.

While watching the dancers perform in the water and the singers move forward to the dancer's edge and back to the "shore," an arc of light appeared, and I saw our entire history of colonization unfold, replete with our absence in the cultural and physical life of the building of two entire continents. There was this aura of murder, then a strange placation of genocide's tension, in which our cultures were attacked and thwarted, then sent into hiding underground in enclaves of tense song and fearful dance, and finally the women burst forward in this magical moment of reclamation that included "the Indigenous Mothers of Africa and America" birthing children who took to the water to reinvent themselves, their history, and their future, not once, but many times over.

At the same time that I am captivated by the story, I cannot take my eyes off the dancers, particularly Penny Couchie and Santee Smith, whose bodies look as though they feel every moment of our history. On the one hand, they dance through the history, and on the other hand, they resist that history in dance so gorgeous I weep. In my mind, I watched my grandmothers, my great grandmothers, hauling McClary stoves across mountain passes, digging clams whose beds were dying, poisoned by toxic waste that was not to be cleaned up for over a hundred years. I watched them feed children consumed with disease and I grieved as I imagined who we might have been if, when the interlopers came, we had been invited back to the table they appropriated from our Ta'ahs. This is who we might have been, magicians bringing the women of three continents together in song and dance.

The spell broke, the procession ended, the singers and dancers exited, and I realized that "we" had done it; Alejandro, Penny, and the dancers had created a piece so impossibly beautiful, so magical, that there we were, culturally part of the world of theatre and dance again, in our own way, conjuring and forging our way into future.

Some additional words after talking with Penny about song, dance, and movement:

"Your whole family is so about movement"

We had berry-picking songs, medicine gathering songs, paddle songs, clam-digging songs, grieving songs, and clan-naming songs, personal songs, love songs, war songs; in short, we had songs for every bit of work and life we engaged. We had healing songs, story songs, songs of gratitude, gambling/ recreation songs, and personal songs of power. We had songs for clowning about and we had dances that went with them. Even our speaking was accompanied by elegant gestures that made our speaking artful. We held that art is "our way of life" and that "everything begins with song." We sang in our living rooms, legal, Western-based songs when they outlawed our original music. We sang in the hop fields and berry fields, songs of love, of hope, blues tunes of hardship, and every song was accompanied by dance and movement: we could not relinquish the belief that the body was made to move; in fact, "stasis," the absence of movement, for us signals the beginning of death. The very moment our songs and dance became legal, we opened the big house, and our elders, crippled and stilled by age, gathered that winter to sing and dance. As audience members, we were expected to tap out the rhythm of the song, sing with the singers, move with the dancers, give them our energy by way of helping them to sing and dance. We were to extend all the energy of our musical selves to the dancer on the floor. We held "sings" to see who had the best "songs," challenged other communities to best our songs. Dance always accompanied the sing and feasting followed. Everyone got up to dance. Our dance movements were simple. They were as simple as the waves of the sea, marking shore, calling us to fish, as elegant as the wind blowing the berry bushes as we picked. Simple as our movements were, they engaged our whole body. We danced as individuals and as collectives assisting the individual. Song and dance was about genuine power, the power within, and the collective movement was a kind of holy coming together of the body of the clan, the village, and the nation. Dance makes the Sto:lo sense of power real.

We didn't get up and stand at attention to sing, we bent forward, pulled the song from the deepest part of the earth, and felt it roll up through our legs, fill our bellies, and roll out to greet the air. Every song was the deepest, most profound sound of our gratitude, our appreciation, our celebration of being, of life, of family, of ancestry, and of our nationhood, and every song was accompanied by movement and dance. Song was cellular, it was about blood, it was about the dynamic clearing of the body of toxicity. Our bodies were so totally engaged in the process of song and dance nearly all the time that it was effortless to walk.

I went to the longhouse at Musqueam during the winter dances when I was eighteen to twenty-four years old. As we entered, we were all given a stick. I walked up to the highest benches where there was a slim space for me to sit. The moment the drums began and the song rolled out, we all tapped in unison without instruction; we leaned into the song and swayed to the music, struggling to give all our energy to the dancer, who shook and shook until her old arthritic body regained its youthful litheness. She leapt into the air and danced about on the dirt floor of the longhouse. Our eyes followed her, our heart followed her, and we felt the urgency of pushing out as much of our strength as we could give her. Our feet tapped, our shoulders rolled, our arms and torsos swayed, our backsides fairly bounced up and down on the benches. After the first few seconds of song and dance, my body felt so light I floated, swayed, moved, and transformed into a slip of barely physical being. I felt invincible, fragile, vulnerable, and strong in the same moment. I felt transformed from the ordinary, disconnected, utilitarian tasks of life into the magic world of Salish being. I carried on all day and into the night, drumming with that stick, bench-dancing with that woman, and singing with the singers. Even today, I can dance for hours, though walking is tiring. As long as I sing, I can carry out the most mundane task tirelessly. Song has carried me through terror, helplessness, grief, pain, work, and stress, and rhythms make short work of labour. My grandfather's family song, now the anthem for people of BC, has saved my life many times.

I went five more years after that and twice while my girls were small. In the intervening years, when I did not attend the longhouse, I grew sick. They say that if we don't go to the longhouse we will become sick. It is not absence from the longhouse that sickens; it is the absence of song and dance in our lives that makes us ill. I decided to sing and dance in my ordinary life, and people chuckle when they see me sway to some inaudible tune going on inside my head, but I can behave in no other way. Song and movement create magic and are so much a part of our world, our life, that we literally cannot be without it. I remember jumping about and dancing around to Hank Williams, Buddy Holly, then later Creedence Clearwater Revival, Wilson Pickett, and Black freedom songs in the days before our music found its way to tape. It took us three decades to recover from the cultural bans and begin to dance in the longhouse again. Another three decades passed before we taped our music, and still I anticipate another three decades before we dance our way through life in the way our ancestors did.

Movement and the signals of the body, its engagement in the speaking process, the way we rock back and forth, step forward and move back, the drum we engage in the telling of story or launching of a boat or gathering food are still with us, but not in any conscious or consistent way. We have the big house as our ceremonial house; it is where the healing songs, the sacred songs, the recalling of the ancestors took place, and we have revived that, but the everyday singing your way through work has suffered, and so our bodies are stiller than they ought to be, and that is the seat of all kinds of disease and neuroses. The stasis of the absence of dance transforms us into toxic waste dumps and fills us with poisoned thoughts and perverts our very soul. Without song, dance, and rhythmic movement, I cannot be a sane person. I know this.

Jogging, pulling weights, skiing—whatever exercise you choose—does not have the same effect as dance. The ripple of the flesh, the working with the natural rhythm of the body, connect the heart mind and spirit together in beauty. Exercise will strengthen, but dance enlivens. Dance speaks to us, stories us up in some longevity of spirit that has no replacement.

I love the ripple of my flesh, the struggle to feel the movement of the hairs across my arms as my skin responds to a drum, whether that drum is hidden under a guitar or is the open raw drumbeat of an Indigenous song. I cherish the feeling in my feet as my body fights for the depth of sound required to sing. I am uplifted by the total engagement of my body in song or dance.

Without movement, I feel a crazy shrinking of the space between the very cells of my body; as the skin contracts, loses elasticity, my body becomes locked, and the light, the blood, the body's very detoxification system inside me begins to slow. Rejuvenation, cell reproduction cannot occur. Without rhythm, we cannot find the lightness of being to fully realize our personal strength and agility, and our willingness to work shrinks as our very desire to experience life begins to die. The fire inside, the breath required to kindle that fire, shrinks, and new life cannot occur, new cells cannot be produced, toxic waste accumulates in the old cells and runs amok, telling the toxic cells to kill themselves, and eventually these instructions meet our minds and we entertain thoughts of suicide or worse, we consider the murder of others to quiet the poisoned being we are consigned to. I believe this.

A good adrenal rush detoxifies the body in a hurry, cleans out the mind, restores some kind of emotional balance missing, and so we fly into crazy adrenal rush rages and take out our madness on our wives, our children, anyone who is handily powerless. Alcohol is the fuel needed to fire up the rage. Our children suffer no end of degradation. I think about this on the heels of Earth in Motion's Harbourfront performance. I consider this in the wake of Penny Couchie's words about how "your whole family is about movement and dance." I think about this as I watch my past unfold behind me, see the sharp stones of trouble on that path, and I watch myself dance my way across the stones, light-stepping through trouble, a song on my lips, and my arms and hips shaking their way forward. I consider how much easier my life has been since the day I decided that I need to shake my way through trouble, I need to break into dance whenever the notion strikes, I cannot afford to censor my body. I danced at every powwow I could, dance every day in my living room, in the living rooms of others, in my place of work whenever I hear the music go off in my mind. It is not the kind of dance that would ever make me a performance-art dancer like the women on the stage of *Agua/Water*, but it is the kind of everyday song and dance that lightens your journey, enlivens your life, and brings you to the promise of the joyful being of living life as art. But that is the ordinariness of having "art as a way of life." It helps you to take the next step in the journey across the stone-filled path that is your life. Humans need and deserve something more. It is the kind of "When all else fails, sing; when you are tired, dance; and song and dance will bring you through," but that is existence, survival, it is not full living. We also need to see our lives danced and sung. We need to create the time and space in which our most talented crafters of song and dance can story up the heroic, significant moments of our history and we need to see our lives danced before us in that spectacular and uplifting way that has always been a part of our lives.

We are also about water: deep water, rushing water, smooth water, and delicate water.

The engagement of song and dance in the recreation of our life is "high art." We had "high art" in our past, the sort of extravagant dance productions that engaged the whole community in watching an unfolding drama of song, dance, healing, ceremony, or story. This high art inspired us to something more than just getting through, just surviving. It inspired us to lead ever-fuller lives. Such dance stories urged us to augment our being, to come to understand our very humanity. I always had the kind of getting through life with dance, but at the same time I needed "high art," the sort of staging of our story, the mask-based theatrical productions of those whose business was the creation of story through song and dance that would move us from survival mode to full life, to an enriched cultural being. That kind of song and dance of high art has been missing for a long time, and I did not know it was missing in my life until I saw Earth in Motion's piece. I missed it, and the missing it created this gnawing hunger for it so deep and so all-encompassing that it filled every cell of my body. I was so full of this terrible hunger for it that it felt normal to be continuously hungry; it became so normal that I did not know life without hunger.

Humans must witness the greatest artistry that their most gifted artists can create.

Earth in Motion's Harbourfront dance showed me how much we needed high art. This form of song, dance, as production showed me that we need high art so that we can witness the procession, the presentation, the unfolding of the drama of our lives from beginning to end in order to feel whole. I need it to know that I belong to a community, to my history, that I am more than a workwoman, a drudge, a survivor. I need it to know I have a cultural history, a cultural being worthy of presentation. I need to know I am present and presented. My body needs to know there is a direct connection between my origin and my current being. I need to know that there is greatness and glory in our history and that we are capable of creating artistic witness of ourselves in the context of history, that our lives are the subject that can and must birth beautiful art. It is not just the collective's responsibility to participate in the creation of this high art; it is the right of the collective to witness those who are gifted and trained to create it. It is the collective's responsibility to ensure that our high art has a place on the stages of Canada. It is my right and responsibility to ensure that the best of Indigenous song/ dance art is presented onstage.

Participating in Columpa Bobb's *Moving Gallery* and having her integrate my poem into the production was one of the highlights of my performance-art career. Participating with Aanmitaagzi and the Train of Thought is another highlight. Finally, participating with Article 11 and Santee Smith and her daughter Semia at the Edinburgh Fringe is another highlight.

This presentation of high art brings us to ourselves in a full and appreciative way: it reminds us that we have danced our way through difficulty on a daily basis, danced our way to song and full life, sang and danced our way to health and well-being, and that the rhythms of our people still sing through every cell in our bodies. I am reminded that we have done so as participants and as witnesses. Great art grabs hold of the crazy-adrenal-rush-madness that sometimes finds its way inside the body and removes it. It cultivates a powerful belonging and from that place of belonging, great being can emerge. It is in our belonging that our desire to contribute to the greatness of our collective being is born. This is the place of witness. We can dance our way through difficulty all by ourselves, but we cannot kindle the fire of our desire to contribute to the collective being of the world without witnessing this high art. A melancholy persists in the individual who has never witnessed themselves through the extraordinary art of their most talented citizens. It is impossible to truly see yourself outside of the best of your national art. It makes us weep with appreciation over the beauty of our finest, most gifted artists, and this weeping fills us with gratitude that we are alive at this moment in our history and proud to witness the journey we have been on, no matter how terrible it has been.

We need this. Our children are on the brink of murder and suicide; they need it. We need to bring ourselves back to full life, to revive our cultural forms of expression and train our kids to create the high art that will inspire them to contribute to their lives, to celebrate their troubles, and to dance their way forward, to sing away their fears and to express themselves in their grief, their work, their being.

Canada and Canadians would do well to learn from us. More art, more song, more dance will bring us to wellness. Cross-cultural dance will get us to know each other. The Train of Thought, the *Moving Gallery,* and Aanmitaagzi's contribution to the Train of Thought are examples of how extraordinary, powerful art can be in the transformation of relations between one another.

The creative mind does not know any stupid questions and often ferrets out great answers.